A spiritualist's journey to find her true calling.

Marti Tote

Marti Tote
RENO, NEVADA

Copyright © 2015 Marti Tote

A Whisper In The Wings
A spiritualist's journey to find her true calling

All rights reserved. No part of this book may be used or reproduced by any means, graphic electronic, or mechanical, including photocopying, recording, taping or by any information storage retrieval system without the written permission of the author except in the case of brief quotations embodied in critical articles and reviews.

Because of the dynamic nature of the Internet, any web addresses or links contained in this book may have changed since publication and may no longer be valid. The views expressed in this work are solely those of the author.

The author of this book does not dispense medical advice or prescribe the use of any technique as a form of treatment for physical, emotional, or medical problems without the advice of a physician, either directly or indirectly. The intent of the author is only to offer information of a general nature to help you in your quest for emotional and spiritual well-being. In the event you use any of the information in this book for yourself, which is your constitutional right, the author assumes no responsibility for your actions.

Any people depicted in stock imagery provided by Thinkstock are models, and such images are being used for illustrative purposes only. Certain stock imagery © Thinkstock.

Printed in the United States

ISBN: 978-1-5087-0996-1

Marti Tote
Reno, Nevada
www.AngelicSensations.com

I dedicate this book to all of us who "Believe."
And in loving memory of my dear friends,
Rebecca Reisig and Shaun Wiggins, who both
made it to the other side before me.
You both swore I was an Angel. And now—
look who has gotten their wings.

Acknowledgments and Special Thanks

THERE ARE MANY friends and family members whom I must thank and acknowledge for their belief in me, as without them, I probably would have never written this book!

To Lindy Brooks, my best friend, my daughter-in-law, and biggest supporter throughout my tireless and continuous journey to reveal who I really am. You have fought my battles, pushed me beyond my limits, and always taken my side when my back was to the wall. Others made fun of me, and you believed in me even when it was difficult. You stuck your neck out for me more times than I can count, which put you in my shoes! You have helped me decorate every one of my session's rooms way into the wee hours of very early mornings and you never told me no. You have been my pillar of strength and courage throughout this entire passage. Through it all—we prevailed and we made it! So to you, Lin—I will be forever grateful, and I love you with all my heart!

To my big sis Jodie, who grew up with a very strange little sister and yet never stopped believing in me—never stopped loving me—and you never tire of listening to me! You taught me how to love others and how to give back what I receive. You have watched me grow and taken my side even when you didn't understand, because you had faith in your little sister. You have fought my battles and pleaded my case more times than I can count, and I love you beyond words. You are me and I am you! We will always be a part of each other, and we will always stand side by side because that's what sisters do!

To my husband, Bob, who listens to me even when you don't understand. You are my lifeline and my "go to" person when the world seems so unfair and the walls are caving in. You have endured more than your share of my gift, and you have never doubted me even when you didn't or couldn't understand. You are my rock and my safety net, and I love you!

To my children: Jason and his wife, Sheena; Michael and his wife, Lindy; Jack and his wife, Kim; Jessica, Donovan, and Bryce. All of you will carry on my story and my legacy long after I am gone. It's quite a heavy torch to carry, but I know without a doubt you will do it with pride and honor! All of you have had to endure some ribbing along this old story road, but you held steadfast, you believed in me, and you have all expressed how proud you are of me. That is the sort of pride that can move mountains—and it has! Thank you, my beautiful and precious children! You are the very light of my heart and soul and the reason I am here! I love you!

To my grandchildren: Kaycee, Cody, Taylor, Dylan, Sean, Zoey, Sweet Wesley James, and Shelbie (wherever you are). You have quite a different grandmother than most, but I promise you all, no matter how different I am, my love for you will always be immeasurable! Once I am gone from this place, it will be up to you to teach the world that life and love do no not end here—they begin here! Always remember that and know that I love you all!

To my friend and fellow writer, Sue Cornfield. For all the hours spent correcting my letters and stories, unselfishly taking time away from your own writing. What a sacrifice. You are an exceptional writer and an even more exceptional friend, and I love you!

To my confidant and closest friend, Julie Krueger. You met me at a time in your life when death had overwhelmingly darkened your doorstep numerous times and made you so afraid to love; you were paralyzed with fear of loss. But you persevered and dared to learn about a world beyond this place. In learning about death—you embraced how to live! You are one of my biggest supporters in spite of the remarks and snickers from others. My gratitude goes far beyond what words can say. I love you, my friend, and thank you!

To Carol Avalos. You offered your own private reading in your own words for this book. Even though I know it was painful for you,

you wanted to share it with my readers to validate my gift. I will never understand how you breathe in and out every day, but you do! You have taught me so much about perseverance, bravery, faith, and facing a heartache that is every mother's worst nightmare! I love you for your unwavering courage, and I am proud to say that I have learned far more from you than you could have ever learned from me!

To my editor, Gail Chadwick, who puts up with my constant need to know everything! Who prepares my words for the world to see and does it with editorial expertise and pride just as she extends her friendship, love, and understanding to me. I think it is perfectly appropriate to say I love you to my editor! And I do! Thank you, Gail! If only we had a penny for every misplaced dash or comma!

To Doreen Virtue. Webster's own words could never describe how grateful I am to you for taking the time to validate my true calling. I will never doubt the existence of true earth Angels, for I have met you!

And last, but certainly not least: To all of my clients (friends), who over the past several years have encouraged me to write this story. Thank you all for pushing me to believe in myself as much as you all believe in me!

Prologue

SALUTATIONS AND WELCOME to my private and sometimes secluded world of the unforeseen and the unknown. Well, to some anyway. It's not unknown to me. It actually never was. However, it was indeed lonely at times? Oh yes—in every sense of the word.

When I decided to take the risk and write this story, my story, it most certainly wasn't an easy decision. I have always hidden who I really am in a "secret squirrel" sort of way; never to reveal my true identity unless I was really needed and there was trouble of some sort. Then, of course, the invisible and many talents of me would come rushing in, thus saving the day! Or something like that? OK—maybe nothing like that, but it surely felt like it. Nice thought anyway.

Throughout the better part of my life I had to conceal my true identify in order to socially survive. So, that part of my life, the part that harbored all of my deepest most hidden treasures has always been a secret. Well, until now.

First of all, I feel it important to say that I have always felt this gift was a blessing. And just for the record, I have never thought of my gift as a curse, *never*. There were times I had no clue what to do with myself, nor did I know what to do with those folks I was seeing and hearing that no one else could see or hear, but I never thought of it as a curse. Perhaps it was inconvenient at times. But a curse? Well, a curse to me sounds like hocus-pocus witchcraft stuff—and I gotta tell you—that's a tough pill to swallow when you hang around with Angels all day long.

As far back as I can remember I always had this gift. I didn't just wake up one day in my life to discover I had it. As far as I am concerned,

I was chosen; it was for some reason gifted to me at birth. I could see folks that others could not see, and I could hear beings that others could not hear. And the more I tried to share and tell about it, the more alone I became. Well, at least here in this place that we call earth. If you ever want to clear a room, just tell someone you are a medium. Of course, I had no clue that is what I was when I began the journey of my life. I wasn't aware there was even a title to my issue until I was much older. Heck, I didn't even know I had an issue at all for that matter! Nonetheless, I learned very quickly and very early on, not to talk out loud about things that others "do not"—or "cannot"—understand or see. Well, that along with religion and politics. All of the above are huge no, nos!

I am about to take you along with me on my quest. One that I would guess actually began back in 1958, which was the year I was born. However, I truly don't recall my birth, nor do I recall any part of my life until I was about three years old. I think that's about status quo for most of us. Anyway, I am more than happy to have your company. I don't have to hide anymore and I am no longer afraid to share *who* or *what* I am. That feels good. It feels freeing.

But it wasn't always that way.

It took me forty-seven long years to actually step out among others and not only admit I was different but be proud that I was different. I am a light worker and a healer of the heart and the mind. Wow, what a badge of honor to have been bestowed, and I now wear it proudly. Getting there was the challenge.

So, sit back, relax, and enjoy this true story of bewilderment, perseverance, shame, pride, gratitude, and miracles. I could probably add many more words; however, this is an introduction to my story, so I will let you fill in the blanks where I left off.

Blessings to you all!

I'm happy to have you along!

Chapter One

Why Me?

Nobody Knows the Trouble I've Seen!

As I begin this story of the unbelievable, I would love to open with a line packed full of great words of wisdom. Words such as: I have all the answers to the mysteries of the universe so don't worry; you are *not alone*. Or perhaps, the unexplainable is always easiest when you have a friend who has been there—or wait—better yet, I have proof that all the unexplainable will now be explained, so just sit back, relax, and enjoy! Yes, indeedy, I would love to begin this story with all those lovely innuendos; however, that would be silly, because just as I have learned, everyone's journey in life is different, and therefore, so are their gifts!

So you see, it doesn't really matter whether or not you are alone, just as much as it doesn't really matter if I felt I could explain the unexplainable or not, because no matter how many people give you their input, and no matter what they think they can prove, they cannot walk your path for you! But the great news is: You really *are not* alone—and although I, myself, can't walk your path for you either, perhaps what I *can* do is ease your mind just a bit. Perhaps, hold your hand and help guide you through this twilight zone of unanswered questions you just may be having.

First of all, and most importantly, if you are reading this book, then something must be happening in your life that you just cannot understand or comprehend and you're looking for answers. Or, perhaps you have had your own experience that you simply just cannot make sense of, or you may simply be curious. Well then, there is more great news in this sea of unanswered questions you have been drowning in. There is probably not a thing wrong with you! Now don't you feel better already? Well you should! Now you don't have to check into *that* hotel that sits high upon the hill on the outskirts of every town, surrounded by barbwire-topped fences. Well, not just yet anyway. Although I have heard it's a lovely place, such a lovely place!

I surely cannot address every reader individually, but what I can do is share my passage with you and perhaps in doing so, I can show you some shortcuts along the way. Maybe I can help you find your own way just as I did. Or I may be able to shed a little light on the unknown. After all, that's what friends are for, right? Or so they say, and therefore—now we begin.

It has been my experience throughout my lifetime to realize that everyone has a story. Yep! EVERYONE! Every one of us has some sort of story trailing behind us, and if we really take the time to listen, they are all truly incredible. I mean, after all, not real sure if you have noticed lately, but this isn't such an easy place to get along in sometimes, this place we all call earth. It can be harsh and cruel, and yet it can also be inviting and wonderful. All in the eyes of the beholder, my friends.

The question I am most often asked is: When did you know you had this gift? Huh, let me ponder that for just a quick little moment here and—the moment is now over and—well, to be quite honest, I'm not real sure. So how do you like that? Uh huh, not so simple for me to answer that question because truth be told, I wasn't real sure that what I had, *was* a "gift," as they called it. I thought that something just had to be wrong with me! Therefore, I simply chalked it up as great intuition. I just always knew that certain someones were yakking at me constantly, and so I chalked *that* up in my pretty little noggin to my unhealthy childhood and perhaps multiple personalities. And quite frankly, I don't know about you, but I sure as heck wasn't going to admit any of that hullabaloo to anyone! Ah, but once again there was a light at the end of my tunnel (pun truly intended), and in about my mid-twenties, I began to realize (admit to myself) that those someones who were hanging around had truly been there for quite some time. OK, in all honesty, my entire life!

As I begin to think back to my earliest recollection as to how long I have been hearing these special and precious someones, my first memory is not just of hearing, but of actually *seeing*! Yes, seeing! Something I promised myself I would never—and I mean *never*—admit out loud to anyone! Uh huh. And here we go! First lesson: *Never* say never!

He was a little boy by the name of Tommy who came to the bathroom with me and only showed up when I was all alone. Now of course I told my parents about this little fellow, and they in turn, of course, simply thought it was so darned cute that little Marti had an imaginary friend, and this was because I lived in a household of all girls. This must have been my way of creating a brother. Now just how cute was that? Huh, boy! About as cute as a bug's ear, as my dad used to say, which I never quite understood even to this day. I have truly always hated bugs, and if I ever in my life saw one with ears I would probably faint!

Tommy first showed up in the bathroom, and I reckon that is because I was deathly afraid of the toilet! My dad would walk me in there, set me atop of every man's throne, and leave me there with my feet dangling until I did my business. That was our job when we were kids; to sit on the toilet and do our business. That is where our business went. And to this day, all due respect, I have to say I agree! All business, for that matter! So, once he set me upon the porcelain god, secured only by my trembling arms with my hands placed tightly on each side of my body, holding on for dear life to the seat of that horrible contraption, my dad would leave and Tommy would immediately show up. He'd be sitting on the edge of the bathtub across from me, and we had wonderful conversations about everything and anything we could possibly think of under the sun! We talked about my fear of the toilet of course, as well as bike riding and the difference between horses and ponies, butterflies and caterpillars, oh, and my parents. Tommy knew my mom wasn't so nice and my dad was my savior. I never had to explain things to him. He just knew all and everything about me, and that made me feel very safe with him. We also spoke quite a bit about my grandfather who lived with us because he was always very sick and that really worried me. Anything at all that came to my mind was what we talked about while I was trying to make my business happen.

Well, well, well. How very comforting that all truly was, except for the one thing that I never really told my parents because I was too young to care to even mention it. Tommy's mouth never moved, and he didn't have a voice! I only heard him in thought, but I spoke to *him* out loud. He was not transparent, and I could clearly see his features. I wasn't one bit intimidated by the fact that he was a boy and I was sitting on a plastic donut seat with my bottom exposed. I was actually quite comfortable with him, and he understood me. I loved him and I know he truly loved me. He was my friend! And that was my first memory of talking to someones who didn't exist to others. I was four years old. The year was 1962.

Average cost of new house $12,500
Average income per year $5,556
Average monthly rent $110 per month
Tuition to Harvard University $1,520
All-Wheel Drive Scout off-road $2,150
Renault imported car $1,395
Average cost of a new car $3,125
Eggs per dozen 32 cents
Gas per gallon 28 cents

The Cold War continued to worsen when the Russians placed ballistic missiles on Cuban land just ninety miles away from the coast of Florida, and JFK called their bluff by threatening war unless they were removed, which they were, but for a short time the world was on the brink of nuclear war and self-destruction.

The president then set a goal of landing a man on the moon before the end of the decade and became more involved in politics in Southeast Asia by training South Vietnamese pilots.

Folk music was evolving into protest music thanks to young artists like Bob Dylan, and surfing music by the Beach Boys grew in popularity. Meanwhile in England, the Beatles recorded the single "Love Me Do."

The new hit on TV for that year was "The Beverly Hillbillies" and the first of the James Bond movies, "Dr. No," was an instant success!

The first US rocket Ranger IV landed on the moon on <u>April 26.</u>

The first ever flavored chips sold as salt and vinegar.

Marilyn Monroe was found dead on <u>August 5</u> after apparently overdosing on sleeping pills.

The first Wal-Mart discount store was opened by Sam Walton in Bentonville, Arkansas.

Johnny Carson began as host of "The Tonight Show."

And nowhere in the events of history reported for that year did anyone ever mention that it had been discovered that I had been blessed with a gift, because those things were not discussed because psychics wore turbans and gazed into crystal balls.

Now I'm quite sure with all the change that was going on in the world at that time, coming up on the heels of the hippie era: free love, peace, rock 'n' roll, and all that other garb, that the last thing my parents needed was their four-year-old daughter talking to, well, I'm not real sure what Tommy was, so let's just call him an entity. I don't like the word ghost—scares the living hoopla out of folks.

So, as I was saying, the last thing my parents needed to deal with was their four-year-old daughter talking to an entity. Thank God or whomever you choose to pray to that I could not explain who Tommy *really was*. Heck, I didn't know myself, nor did I care. I was just darn glad he was there!

From that time forward in my life, I truly can't remember ever being alone. And I don't remember the day Tommy left me, just as I cannot remember the day he arrived. I feel as though he had just always been there. And I'm glad I do not remember his departure. Makes me feel extremely sad now, so I can't imagine the separation anxiety I must have experienced when he left me back then. In all honesty, at that time we lived in an old farmhouse in Canton, Ohio, on about twenty acres, and I don't remember him going with us when we moved from that old house. So perhaps, just perhaps, Tommy lived there long before we did and perhaps, just perhaps, he didn't want to leave. Maybe he couldn't. I truly don't know. What I do know is that I lost the one person who knew me inside and out and I would never again be the same. Of course, we never really are the same from one day to the next. Of course not! Because the world is forever changing; therefore, so are we. And I will tell you that whether we lose a person to death or to the end of a relationship, or the person simply moves away or leaves our lives for one reason or another, or we leave that person's life, we are never, and I mean *never*, the same again. People leave imprints on our hearts forever, whether we have known them for just a few minutes or for our entire lives. It's just that some leave a deeper imprint than others, and I find that to be truly amazing as you will see as we travel down this old story road. I have known folks that I met for only a few minutes in a grocery store that left a bigger imprint on my heart than some folks I have known all my life. Now doesn't that just make you think? Well it should, because it's all in the plan!

Tommy was not the only something or someone I remember seeing. Uh no! That would have made this story much too simple, well, and short. I saw so many others around me that if my parents had known, they may have succumbed to heart attacks, and I would have been orphaned at a very young age!

During that time of my life, I truly knew in my heart of hearts, that wishes really could come true! I would close my eyes real tight and wish for things that would make me happy. I can't tell you how many times I would close my eyes as tight as tight could be—and wish for a pony! Then I would open them—and—no pony! Time and time again I practiced and practiced but to no avail! No matter how many times I went through this ritual, it never produced me a pony! That truly bummed me out! So I figured I should stick to praying. I simply figured that if anyone could conjure me up a pony, God could! So I began praying instead of wishing. And—one summer, out of nowhere, my dad did indeed come home with a pony. And once that happened, I knew I had found the secret to prayer! So, I simply decided to pray for more invisible friends. And those I received as well! Oh, and for the record, my dad *did not* bring *them* home!

I saw animals that no one else could see. I saw men and women dressed in old-fashioned clothing. I saw field workers, and I saw children and played with them in the apple orchards behind our home. And the beauty of all this was that I was never alone. That is the beauty of this entire story because neither are you! No one is! Although I felt secluded; I was different, and I knew it.

I always knew when it was *one of them* and mostly because they spoke to me only through my thoughts. Even at my young age I knew not to ask if anyone else could see them. Though I was just a child, I knew exactly who *they* were, where *they* came from, and I was not afraid. Nor did I feel the need to share their existence with anyone. They were *my* friends. I didn't really care if anyone else could see them. I actually preferred that they not. I always felt the need to protect them and keep them a secret. If they wanted everyone else to see them, then they would have visited *them*! Although, my big sis would watch me while I was out playing and even though she, herself, couldn't see them, she never doubted that *someone* was there. She knew I was indeed seeing, talking to, and playing with someone whom no one else could see or hear. It fascinated her and sometimes it really creeped her out. She would come to get me for supper, and I wouldn't want to come right away, so she would take me by the hand and walk me to the house from the yard or the corn fields or the apple orchards, and as she did so, she would get a little bit of a pep in her step as she would look around, walking just a bit faster with me in tow. She is only three years older than I, and she shares with me now that she swears she could feel them watching her. Poor thing. Had I been in that situation, I would have left her butt right there where she had been playing and simply forgotten I had a sister!

My favorite time was bedtime. After my parents would tuck me in and turn out the lights, I would say my "Now I lay me down to sleep" prayer. Then I would sit up in my bed, prop my pillow up behind me, and simply wait for my friends to arrive. I don't know who all those folks were who came to see me, but I always enjoyed their comforting visits. A lot of elderly people hung around me at that time in my life. Late at night in my bedroom, it was mostly the elderly who would come. I really and truly loved that. Sometimes, I would be in my room awake for hours upon countless hours listening and talking to my friends. My aunt tells me that she distinctly remembers playing cards late at night with my parents, and I would come shuffling into the kitchen from my bedroom in my little feet pajamas asking for a drink of water. My dad would ask why I was still awake, and I would try to tell him that my friends were in my room but that only prompted him and my mother to get up quickly from their chairs ushering me out of the kitchen before anyone else could hear me. Then it began. The talks about my wild imagination and how lying was not nice and how it just had to stop! So I guess I listened, or *they* did, because sadly, one day they simply came no more. Well, not that I could see anyway, ah, but I could always feel and hear them. Always!

So from that detrimental time in my life and for just the next few years or so after that, I always spoke to them, I could always feel them around me, and I could always hear them, but I wouldn't actually see them. Problem was I just didn't know who *THEM* was. But it truly didn't matter. I felt safe with them around me. And about the only way I can explain it is, well, it's like when you walk into a dark room and you know there is a piece of furniture there. You can't see it, but you feel its existence. That is how it has been all my life. They are all around me and at least now I know who *they* are. Sometimes, it gets so crowded, I feel as though I am in a shopping mall trying to walk around people that no one else can see. I have to ask them to slow down when they talk too fast, and when I am alone, I always talk out loud to them. They are my Angels and other people's Angels and they are the dead who have crossed over, and quite frankly they have a lot to say. They all have different personalities and different messages. And I have never met an entity I didn't like. I had finally come to the realization that *they* had chosen *me* and that they weren't going anywhere. They would be with me for life! And the only question I had, once I understood this wonderful fact was, why me? However, as I sit here writing this story and as I look back upon my life, I think I have figured it out. They knew what was coming, and I didn't! They always do!

Chapter Two

Don't Tell!

I Won't—If You Don't

I LOST MY ability to *see* entities the year I began first grade. I felt them and I heard them, but I truly don't remember seeing them anymore. I believe they faded away from all those talks my mom had with me about lying and my wild imagination. I may never know why they stopped appearing. And I stopped telling! I didn't want to be a bad person who lied. I didn't want to be a storyteller! Perhaps that is why I suck at writing fiction. I just didn't want God to be ashamed of me. Yes, God. I knew all about God. Before my daddy left our forever home, we went to church every Sunday. And although my vision of God has changed considerably throughout the years, I still believe there is someone out there driving the bus!

I think my dad always knew about my problem (gift) because years later I would learn that his mother, my Gammy, had it too. They say— *they* meaning those folks with more credentials than I—it sometimes skips a generation. Huh, how comforting that should truly be, but it isn't. However, I felt less intimidated when I was around my father. He was such a happy little fellow and everything was so very simplistic in his world. I'm thinking that is because he must have known—something! Yes, he must have had some sort of a clue that his cute, little, chubby, chatty daughter had some sort of *thing* going on in her pretty little head.

One of my fondest memories are of us walking up those brick Baptist church steps and him taking his stogie out of his mouth and laying it on the brick ledge right outside the doors so he could retrieve it when we exited God's house. And I realio trulio believed that it *was* indeed, God's house. Just could never figure out why God was never there. You know? Why wasn't he the one out greeting us when we came in? It was, after all, *HIS* house. Never really made any sense whatsoever at all to me! My dad, of course, always had an explanation for everything, so when I asked him about this nagging concern of mine, he quite simply told me that just like Santa had helpers, well, so did God. Huh. I wasn't buying that for a minute, not even a second, because when I prayed, I could hear *Him* too. It wasn't as often as I heard my other friends, but I know I felt and heard "The Boss!" God was the boss of all the Angels. I knew this, it was a given. Like a big fat duh of all duhs in little kid history!

The story I had been taught in Sunday school about that guy Moses up on that mountain was enough for me! He had to turn his face away because God was just too bright to look at, so what was the use? End of story! I simply reckoned that God just wasn't meant to be seen.

I must have done something terribly wrong in church at one time or another, because just after my dad would set that cigar down on the brick ledge, right outside of God's dwelling, he would then always turn to me and stoop down to wipe my little black patent leather shoes (that were never dirty) and as he did, he would give me the speech.

"Now don't tell Mrs. So and So that her husband is talking to you, OK?" he would plead. "If they talk to you, just keep it to yourself."

"Why?" I would ask him.

"They want to talk to the people they love," I would reason. But my dad told me that it upset people when I did that. This little ditty confused me more than ever. Why in the world would my friends upset anyone? But, when you love your dad, and he takes the time to wipe off your shoes when they surely weren't even dirty just to give you a warning—well, when you are a little kid, you respect that. So, I would enter God's house and even though I felt bum rushed by all my friends, some new and some old, I would keep my mouth shut. And sometimes it really hurt my feelings, because I felt as though my unseen friends didn't understand. I felt as though I was letting them down and to this day, if it happens in a grocery store or wherever I might be in public, I realize my dad was probably preparing me for the rest of my life, whether he knew it or not. I mean, after all, I can't just walk up to strangers and say a deceased loved one wants to talk to them. I mean, I guess I could, and quite frankly, I actually *have*, as you will find out later on; however, I think it is very socially unacceptable behavior. But the problem is they do! They always do. They always want to talk or visit or just say, "Hey, I'm here!" And sometimes—not always but sometimes—they tell me when they are preparing a place for someone. Yes, sometimes they warn me that someone is going to leave this place. Those are the toughest of all messages. And I keep those messages to myself most of the time.

I still had no clue at that time in my life that some of these folks had crossed over. Because when you are a kid, you think that everyone who goes to heaven becomes an Angel, so I simply thought all of them were Angels. It wasn't until much later in my life that I realized there is indeed a significant difference between an Angel and the dead. But this is now, and we are still on then.

My incredible need to share information became increasingly worse as I grew older. It got so intense that my dad had to bribe me before entering God's house. If I was quiet and didn't talk to anyone *here* or *there*, he would take me home by way of the Amish country and I could look at the big field horses. But only if I stayed quiet! Boy, was that a chore! Especially for me! But I did it because I loved those big work horses that I now know are Belgian draft horses. I have owned one for many years. And although I have loved and lost a few of them throughout the years, there is always a Belgian in my barn. So thanks, Dad!

I would squirm in church like crazy, partly because I wanted to scream out to every person within the confines of "God's house" that their loved ones had something to say, and partly because I couldn't wait for our drive home. We would get out of church and my dad would reach for that cigar that was faithfully waiting for him right where he had left it, and we would head for the car, and I knew what I was going to see. My mom and dad took separate cars to church for this very reason. Of course I wouldn't know this until many years later. I simply thought my mom couldn't put up with my constant yakking like my dad could, which was true as well, but not the main reason they took separate cars to church.

My dad would drive different back roads each Sunday and we would find a field where the work horses would be grazing, because Sunday was their day off. We would pull over, park, and I would hop out of the car. My dad would pick me up and set me on the hood of the car, and I would simply watch them. Watch them and dream. They were the most magnificent creatures I had ever laid my eyes on! Sometimes they would come to the fence but not very often. They were work horses and they weren't very social. I would tell my dad that someday I was gonna own me one of those big horses. A big red one with a blond mane and tail, and he would ask me what in the world was I going to do with it? And I very knowingly with a satisfying nod said, "I'm gonna ride 'em and drive 'em in my own buggy." My dad always told me I couldn't ride those big horses. You would look like a pea on a mountain, he would say. Well, I'm here to tell you I ride and drive them, and I probably do look like a pea on a mountain, but I'm a happy pea! And that's all I have to say about that.

On our way to the Amish Country on those Sunday mornings, as soon as I got in the car I never shut up. All of my friends would be talking to me, and I would talk back. Sometimes I was angry with them for talking to me in church. "I told you to be quiet," I would say to them. That is when my dad began the ritual of offering me pennies for every minute I could be quiet in the car, but I never made a dime. My dad said I talked so fast he couldn't understand a word I said. I find that to be quite normal though, as I was talking to several someones at one time. But once we pulled into our driveway, I wasn't allowed to talk out loud to them anymore. It upset my mother. But that didn't matter to me. I could talk to them through my thoughts and they could talk to me the same way. I was six years old. The year was 1964.

Average cost of new house $13,050
Average income per year $6,000
Gas per gallon 30 cents
Average cost of a new car $3,500
Loaf of bread 21 cents
United States postage stamp 5 cents
Average monthly Rent $115
Ticket to the movies $1.25

US Congress authorized war against North Vietnam.
President Lyndon Johnson declared the War on Poverty campaign.
The Warren Commission reported on the assassination of President John F. Kennedy and concluded that Lee Harvey Oswald acted alone.
Students stormed the administration building and staged a sit-in at the University of California. Eight hundred were arrested.
Cassius Clay beat Sonny Liston on February 25 for the world heavyweight championship.
The Boston Strangler was captured.
The first Ford Mustang from Ford Motor Company was made.
Washington, DC, residents were able to vote in a presidential election for the first time.
The most powerful earthquake in US history at a magnitude of 9.2, struck South Central Alaska.

And nowhere in the events of history reported for that year did anyone ever mention the fact that I was forbidden to talk about my gift any longer.

"Don't tell," became my way of life in more ways than one. I became ashamed somewhere along the way to admit that I could talk to invisible people. At one point in time, as I grew older, I even stopped telling my dad. I was only eight years old when he left home so that was probably why more than anything. Yes, I believe that my friends became more intense and very consuming when my dad left home. Perhaps it was because I was getting older, and I just wouldn't let go. Or perhaps it was because my mom had found a boyfriend who moved in with intentions that no human being should ever have. And this was when I became more intuitive than ever. You see, as I shared with you in the last chapter, my invisible friends knew what was coming. During the next phase of my life, I was about to not only see them again, but I would be meeting my very own Angels face-to-face for the very first time.

Chapter Three

Where Are You?

Come Out, Come Out—Wherever You Are!

Throughout my years of conducting readings, my clients have asked me, if there is a God and Angels, why they allow bad things to happen? Why in the name of God himself, would he take people's children or allow people to live through car accidents only to be in a wheelchair for the rest of their lives? Well, as I said in the beginning of this story, I sadly don't have all the answers. I have, however, learned throughout my life and through my communication with the other side that everything is in Divine Order as well as Divine Timing and that God doesn't make mistakes. Of this, I know to be true. If it is your time to go, then by God (pun once again truly intended) you are going. If it isn't, well then fate will intervene. (*Now let me make it perfectly clear that this is my belief, and in no way is it my intention to persuade you. Also, please know that of all the sorrow I deal with every day in my session's room—if I don't believe this—I will lose my mind. Because there is no other way I can justify losing a six-year-old to cancer or a mother of four who is killed in a head-on collision on her way home from work. I have to believe in something, anything at all, to make sense in a world that we don't always understand. And, it probably wouldn't be a bad idea if you did the same. You know, keep the old sanity in check!*

First of all, it is my belief that we cut our own deals before we get here and that we won't remember *why* until we ourselves cross back over, and then it will be the Ah Ha moment of all Ah Ha moments as we know them. Until then, fate as well as faith is what we will live with. Fate created by our own choices. That is what I believe déjà vu is. I believe we are shown many scenarios of the lives we can choose from and we pick one before we get here. So when we have a déjà vu moment, it is because somewhere deep inside that part of our minds that scientists say we don't use, we recall a certain segment of what we were shown, thus the familiarity. So why then, would we not just pick a grand life full of money and no pain and worries? Great question—and I haven't a clue in snow's hell besides the fact that perhaps we chose our lives that we are now living because we have no fear on the other side, nor do we feel pain or understand the ways of this world. I also believe that our lives aren't always about our own lessons but that we are to intervene and become a part of someone else's lesson. Now that's a tough pill to swallow, isn't it? And believe you me, no one had a tougher time understanding this than I did once that monster moved in with us!

He began "having his way with me" when I was nine. Just like "doing my business," that was what they called it in those days. The word molestation was not used. But you know, they may as well have called it murder, because that is what happens to your soul when your insides are ripped apart by a monster before you even understand the facts of life. And to make matters even worse, you aren't allowed to tell a single soul. My father had left home. My mother went on autopilot that year, and I'm not sure if she ever came out of it. And my Angels went on some sort of sabbatical. The year was 1967.

Average cost of new house $14,250
Average income per year $7,300
Average monthly rent $125
Gas per gallon 33 cents
Average cost of a new car $2,750
Movie ticket $1.25

Polaroid <u>makes camera history</u> $50
Parker pen set $11.95

The federal minimum wage is increased to $1.40 an hour.
Race riots broke out in a number of cities in the United States, including Cleveland, Newark, and Detroit.
Interracial marriage was declared constitutional by the Supreme Court in the Loving v. Virginia case and barred Virginia, and by implication other states, from making interracial marriage a crime.
The first Rolling Stone Magazine *was published.*
The first Super Bowl, played between Green Bay Packers and the Kansas City Chiefs, was played with Green Bay winning 35–10.
Jimmy Hoffa began an eight-year prison term for defrauding the union and jury tampering.
A series of tornadoes struck the Chicago area killing more than sixty and creating millions of dollars' worth of damage.
The twenty-fifth amendment to the Constitution was ratified. It dealt with succession to the presidency.
Strikes by teaching staff throughout the country demanded pay increases to keep pace with inflation.
Thurgood Marshall became the first black justice on the Supreme Court.
Muhammad Ali was stripped of his heavyweight title for refusing induction into the US Army.

And nowhere in the events of history reported for that year did anyone ever mention that I had my innocence ripped from me by a monster and that I would feel abandoned by my invisible friends!

Yes indeed, that was a tough year to say the least. And I remember wondering where did everyone go? "Where are you, God?" became my prayer at night and I became angry. Angry with God and my Angels for allowing all the bad things that were happening to me, happen. I felt abandoned by everyone! I hardly ever saw my dad. My mom had checked out and went to places unknown in her own mind, and I just couldn't feel them as much anymore. I became frightened for the very first time in my life and uncertain about *everyone* and *everything*. But you know, for some unknown reason, I never stopped praying! As I lay in bed at night preparing for the inevitable to happen, I prayed for them not to leave me. It became obvious that for some reason, they weren't going to stop him. Well, at least they hadn't yet anyway, and I didn't understand this. Why in my greatest time of need had they just left me? And seven long years would go by, as my gift would strengthen beyond even my own understanding.

As I look back now, I realize that they were indeed there. *I* had been the one, in all honesty, who had turned my back on *them*. I don't fault myself for this and neither should you! I was a kid. Even now, in my adult life, I don't always understand the ways of the other side. Perhaps when you spend every second of your free time praying for someone to die; *they* truly don't know how to help. That would be my guess now. But then, back then, all I could do was blame them. Where had they all gone in my most desperate moments of need? And why in the name of God, or whomever you pray to, were they allowing these horrible things to happen to me? And all I have to say to that is—well, I haven't a clue in the name of heaven! But I had indeed been convinced that they had abandoned me in the most crucial and desperate time of my life.

I am embarrassed to say it—but I have to for the sake of telling this story—I have also questioned their existence many times in my adult life as well. I'm not real sure but I think it is normal, whatever normal is, and that sometimes—I'm not real sure, but I'm pretty sure—I think they have a plan. And to complicate this thought process even more, I believe it is called faith. Ah yes, faith! That mystical, magical word that changes meaning as we go merrily, or not so merrily, through our entire lives. You gotta have faith! That is what our Baptist preacher shouted at us every one of those blessed Sunday mornings! Oh, and I never did understand all that yelling either. My dad said he was just passionate in his beliefs. I myself think he was trying to convince folks to believe what *he* believed and he felt like he had to yell to do it. My book, my story, my opinion!

So, let us recap a bit, shall we? Yes, I felt abandoned and lost, and I had stopped praying. I was angry with God and my Angels. Huh, cannot imagine why they had pulled back. Well, unless you take into consideration that those folks on the other side don't much care for anger, or the feeling of hate. Perhaps it makes 'em a little leery. Perhaps it makes 'em pull back so that we will readjust our attitude, belief, and the big one, faith! Hum. Perhaps. Sure does give us all something to think about now, doesn't it? Kind of like that person who wrote "Footprints in the Sand." In our darkest hours, when we feel so alone, could someone be carrying us and we not even know it? Could we be missing the fact that there is only one set of footprints in the sand for a reason?

Chapter Four

We Are Right Here

Just Open Your Eyes!

During the seven years with the monster, I would witness many evils done by this horrible man. Many broken bones and bruises, and murder of my beloved pets, as well as my very soul, would take place. And although history does not report those years as the great depression, I myself absolutely do! I was about to turn fourteen and the year was 1972.

Average cost of new house $27,550
Average income per year $11,800
Average monthly Rent $165
Cost of a gallon of gas 55 cents
Roxanne ladies swimsuit $30
Kodak pocket camera history *$28*
Wrangler jeans $12
Ladies Timex watch from $30.00

HBO was launched in the United States as the first subscription cable service. Richard Nixon ordered the start of the space shuttle program.
  Apollo 16 landed on the moon where the Lunar Rover was tested by astronauts John W. Young and Charles M. Duke.

Apollo 17 landed on the moon, and the last men to walk on the moon were Harrison Schmitt and Eugene Cernan.

Digital watches were introduced.

The first scientific hand-held calculator (HP-35) was introduced (price $395).

The Volkswagen Beetle became the most popular car ever sold with in excess of fifteen million sold.

Atari kicked off the first generation of video games with the release of PONG, the first game to achieve commercial success.

American swimmer Mark Spitz won a record seven gold medals in the Summer Olympics in Munich.

Governor George Wallace was shot three times in an attempted assassination attempt by Arthur Bremer which left him paralyzed.

The Equal Rights Amendment, which provided for the legal equality of the sexes, was passed by the US Senate on March 22.

Hurricane Agnes killed 117 on the US East Coast on June 13.

Five White House operatives were arrested for burglarizing the offices of the Democratic National Committee: the start of the Watergate scandal.

And nowhere in the events of history reported for that year did anyone ever mention that my invisible friends would once again be visible!

By the time I entered my early teens, I had taken on the role of the monster's wife. My big sis had fled home at the age of sixteen and our mother, still gone to places unknown (in more ways than one), worked two full-time jobs, so I was left there alone with that beast of a human being.

This entire horror story will be told in my next book so I don't want to get off track here. The point is, well, that I'm not real sure if there is a point! But this would be the year that I would not only witness *their* rescue of me, but I would see them—*actually see them*—my precious Angels, and I would never forget it for the rest of my life! Nor would I ever share this experience with anyone—until now.

The monster had a schedule and a daily ritual that had to be followed. I got up in the mornings and began my chores, stopped long enough to eat breakfast, then did more chores, stopped to eat lunch and then after lunch we would take a nap.

I was coming into the summer where it would all soon come to an end, but I had no way of knowing this at the time. I was simply a robot.

So there I was, lying underneath him one hot summer afternoon, with my mind wandering to places far away from where I really was just as I always did, and it happened. Up in the corner of my parents' bedroom I saw them! They were not floating, but it seemed as though the three of them were, well, sitting on a swing, although I don't recall seeing the swing, I simply knew it existed.

I heard *her* voice first. It was a woman and two younger little fellas, one on each side of her. She was whispering to my thoughts that they had not left me and that my time was coming.

Oh my gosh, I was so relieved, for I thought she meant I was going to die, and quite frankly, well, I was plain and quite simply relieved. Sad but true. The hope of my mother ever leaving this horrible person had left long ago and been buried and forgotten. And to me, quite frankly, dying simply meant going to heaven, being with God, and that we no longer existed in this place. So I was good with that! Truly I was!

She was so very beautiful and the two little fellas, one on each side of her were, well, Angelic! She gazed at me with a knowing in her eyes. Not really sad eyes, but just understanding. As though she was clearly aware of what I was feeling. Yes, I absolutely knew she understood and well, it comforted me. I asked her when. When would I be leaving? She smiled as she slightly tilted her head and whispered her thoughts back to me—for me to have faith and be patient. Her smile was magical as she caressed the two sitting beside her. They never spoke to me. Only she did. And like Tommy, her lips never moved. But unlike Tommy, she was transparent. I could see the corner of the room through her. She had a slight glow around her. I was so happy to see her. I was so comforted by their presence. I had no awareness as to what was happening to me on that bed. Only them.

"Where have you been?" I asked through my thoughts, with the tears of relief now streaming down my cheeks, and she tilted her head again as if to imply, silly girl, and then she told me: "We have always been here. We have never left you."

"But you did!" I argued.

Yes, I was challenging an Angel! I was actually questioning an Angelic Being!

"No," she whispered gently to my thoughts. "You must forgive him and you must forgive yourself *and* your mother."

What in the heck had she just said? Oh heck no! Was this Angelic crazy person out of her ever-loving feather-flaunting mind? I furrowed my brow, and I told her I could not! I *would* not! How dare she! How dare she not be on my side! With that, she simply whispered, "Ah yes, but you will, you will forgive him."

Well, uh, ah no! I was real sorry for that nice Angel Lady but NO! I absolutely *would* and *could* not *ever* forgive nor forget what this monster had done to me! So as sad as that may have made her, That Little Miss Scarlett O'Hara with a halo and wings, it was not going to happen! Ever! Not in my lifetime anyway! Well, or so I thought at the time anyway.

And I remember no more.

I don't recall when or how they left that day, nor do I recall ever seeing the three of them in my life ever again. Ah, but I felt them and to this day, I still do. And I know it is them. They have become a permanent part of me. They probably always were, as it has been my experience to know that we are never alone. Which would explain why we don't feel silly when we are physically alone and we talk to ourselves. If you think about it, the only time we feel silly talking to ourselves, is when someone else can hear us. Otherwise, we are quite comfortable doing so. Enough said. Some of us may admit this and some of us may not. Nonetheless, I know it to be true! Once again, my book so I get to make up all the rules!

Now before I end this delightful and uplifting chapter, I need to let you all in on another little secret. Throughout this entire ordeal, meaning the seven years of my life that this horrible monster lived with me, I realized I could read *him*. I could tell when there was going to be trouble, and I knew where he was at all times. And always when he was in front of me, I could hear his thoughts. It would be many years to come before I would actually realize that we all have Angels, and all I was doing was hearing his Angels. And I suppose that even the darkest of humans have Angels. I also suppose that those poor heavenly beings truly have their work cut out for them. I mean really, the thought of Charles Manson or Jeffrey Dahmer having Angels is absurd! But I swear to you that I know we are all born with guides! And just because we choose not to follow them, surely doesn't mean they don't exist.

I used to think it was because of the lit cigarette that was forever protruding from the monster's lips that I could feel and know where he was, but I came to know otherwise as I got older. So as I felt and learned, but didn't really understand what I knew, I could stop a situation before it began. I could actually intervene! It didn't always work. Ah, but when it did, I knew it, and it was priceless! However, at the time, I simply thought I was magic! Yes, magic indeed!

Chapter Five

The Gift Becomes Stronger

And All I Ever Wished For—Was a Pony!

After that afternoon, I realized that I was indeed hearing someones whom no one else could hear, and I was also going places other than where I *was* physically while I was wide awake. I could see in my mind scenarios of memories that weren't my own. Not future—But past occurrences of someone else's life! Later on in life—much later—I would learn that that particular gift would prove to be invaluable—but at the time, I simply thought I was nuts!

And that isn't all I realized that grave summer. Oh heck no! That would have made my life a heck of a lot more bearable had it simply stopped there! But it didn't. Because you see, I realized that there were other folks hanging around. Folks who *were not* Angels. Folks who had lived and been here long before me. Folks who could tell me how they had lived here in this place and—how they died! For the very love of Pete! Like I truly needed just one more Godforsaken thing to make me feel nuttier than I already felt! Well, my friends, I reckon I did because it happened. Actually—all that happened was I learned that Angels are much different from those who have crossed over. And thinking back now, I find it amazing that it didn't scare the living hoopla right out of me! But you know, it didn't. I wasn't afraid at all. I was fascinated! Fascinated by their stories, memories, and how they could show me their memories in my mind. They were the same friends from long ago in my childhood bedroom. Only difference was I just didn't see them anymore. I could only feel them and hear their thoughts and see their memories.

I became frustrated because some of them wanted me to go to their loved ones so they could speak to them. Now how in the heck was I supposed to accomplish that task? My dad had already told me each Sunday before church *not* to do that! Not to mention the fact that I had no clue as to how to find their loved ones! And that is when I learned to ask them—tell them—they would have to somehow bring their loved ones to me! And that would be another lesson: Be ever so careful what you ask for! The year was 1973.

Average cost of new house $32,500
Average income per year $12,900
Average monthly rent $175
Cost of a gallon of gas 40 cents
AMC Javelin car $2,900
A dozen eggs 45 cents

Roe v. Wade made abortion a US Constitutional right.
Chrysler and other US car makers closed a number of plants, affecting one hundred thousand workers.
World Trade Center in New York became the tallest building in the world.
Watergate Hearings began in the United States Senate, and President Richard Nixon told the nation, "I am not a crook."
In a tennis match billed as the battle of the sexes—Billie Jean King defeated Bobby Riggs.
Secretariat won the Triple Crown, becoming the first Triple Crown winner in twenty-five years.
Skylab, the first US space station, was launched.
Concorde cut flying time across the Atlantic in half, flying at an average speed of 954 mph.
The Sears Tower opened in Chicago.

Inventions, Inventors, and Countries (or attributed to first use)
Genetic Engineering USA by S. Cohen and H. Boyer
Barcode USA
Optical Fiber USA
Space Station USA Skylab
   Jet Ski, or personal watercraft, was invented by Clayton Jacobson II. The original was a stand-up model and difficult to stay on, manufactured by Kawasaki.

And—nowhere in the events of history reported for that year did anyone ever mention that I would get a calling! And it wasn't Avon!

The rest of that summer went very quickly. The monster was arrested for abusing my mother, shortly after my Angelic friends came to visit me, and we packed up and moved from Southern California to Northern California. And for the record, I told the authorities what the monster had done to me; however, no one at that time in history really gave a rip about such things. But—that is another book, another time, another chapter in my life. Also for the record, my Angelic friend truly meant what she had said to me that day in the bedroom; it *was indeed* almost over.

Shortly after we moved, I began to notice other things happening around me. My friends at school would come to me with their problems, and out of my mouth would come answers. And I mean answers that were—well—right on the money. And I knew darn well that I was simply reporting what I was hearing. I knew those were not *my* answers. They were coming from *that other place*. That is all I knew. *That place* where I could always feel safe when I allowed myself to go there. And I still feel safe going there to this day and probably always will. I knew I could hear and feel other people's Angels! And I knew that little ditty because when I asked, they told me!

It was so noisy in my mind and yet, I knew exactly who was talking to me! Heavenly Beings. And I knew about things beyond any doubt. Through trial and error I learned to ask them to slow down so I could better understand them, and I would ask what messages they needed me to deliver. Unfortunately, these conversations would take place only when someone else was standing in front of me so, to the unsuspecting ever-so-lucky someone who might have been standing in front of me, I probably looked like the RCA dog as I cocked my head and allowed myself to go to distant places in my mind. And then I would repeat what I was being asked to repeat. It would seem to everyone else that I could read them, but to me, I was simply delivering messages. I was just a reporter. And I still am, just a reporter, to this day. However, this created problems for me because even though I was accurate and helpful, I was also snickered at behind my back and labeled as a freak.

I was a heavy teenager, sad most of the time, and very shy. I had horrible acne and had no clue how to dress like the other, more popular, girls in school because my mom didn't have the money to buy me new clothes. So I got what we could afford, which wasn't much, which meant I had to wear the same clothes a few times in the same week, and they certainly were not in style. I'm sure on some level it taught me something. What—I surely didn't know then—but I know now. To this day I am my own person. One-of-a-kind Marti. And I still get snickered at behind my back, but my clothes are not the reason. And you know what? I don't care!

It wasn't until later on in my life, about my mid-thirties or so, I realized I had been graced with yet another sign. I felt the company of an energy coming to my right side, and they would tell me things that could only be described as loving thoughts with an attachment and a familiar memory, and I knew all too well that I was not hearing from an Angel. I could feel *who* that person had been, here in this place, and I could actually take on some of the person's physical characteristics, or I would talk like the person did when he or she was here in this place. That is when I knew something else was happening to me. I wouldn't always get a name but I would know who he or she was to the person standing in front of me, and I always knew how the person had crossed over. And quite frankly—well—I didn't like it! Those feelings can be a bit overwhelming, especially if they needed me to deliver a *specific* message. It can sometimes feel like I'm in some sort of pressure chamber. However, I have learned that if I ask something of them, they will usually accommodate me quite readily. What a novel concept. Ask and ye shall receive! I had to learn to ask them not to get too close to me. It made me feel as though I was being squeezed. Like I couldn't breathe. I have learned throughout the years that it is appreciation. They are thanking me, and they want to touch me. It's a nice gesture, but I believe their energy is what makes me feel like I can't breathe. I honestly feel as though my heart is going into arrest.

So I had come to learn that I felt other people's Angels around them, usually behind them, and their deceased loved ones always came to my right side. Now just exactly what does one do when such a happening occurs? I mean, how in the world do you make sense of such things? Well, I'm not real sure that any of this makes any sense at all. But it works. Yes, it most certainly does. I don't know how computers work either, but they do. And I don't know how the television works, but it does as well. And so—it is written.

I wanted to ask the person standing in front of me if he or she had lost a father or brother or whomever was identifying himself or herself to me, but then I would have gotten *that* look in return. The look of undeniable confusion and fear that says: What in the heck made you ask me that? Then would come the question: How could you know that? Which would in turn, scare the living hoopla right out of me— quite frankly because it made me feel like—well—a freak! Like I had just done something terribly wrong. Sad but true. So I simply stopped asking after a few tries. I didn't want to feel that way anymore and I was already pretty much friendless. So I learned to keep it to myself. For many years I tucked it away. Oh I still spoke with the other side, but I shared it with no one. Sad, huh? All those people who missed out on what their deceased loved ones had to say to them. I am so sorry for all those lost conversations. I truly am.

As I grew older, it of course did not stop. It only got stronger. *The gift*. I surely didn't see it as a gift at the time and, you know, I still don't actually. Well not the way most would think anyway. You see, I consider it a gift for sure but it is *their* gift to me. I am honored that *they* trust *me* with their messages to be delivered to their loved ones. Nonetheless, I became very withdrawn for the next few years. I felt as though no one could possibly understand what I was going through. And I surely didn't take the risk to tell anyone either. Not even my big sister Jodie. It tired me to talk about it and I didn't know *how* to talk about it anyway. What if I made it all up? What if I *was* just a great storyteller like my mom had always claimed?

I had no clue there were books written about such things at that time. And besides, what would they be called? I talk to dead people? I was young, I had been graced with a gift, and I had no clue what to do with it. I just felt different. I felt like my unseen friends were the only ones who could help and understand me, and all *they* wanted me to do was talk to other people! Huh boy!

I left home at the age of fifteen when my mother moved another boyfriend in. I knew it was definitely time to go. I was married by the time I was sixteen and had my first child by the time I was seventeen. I had begun to live my life with the freedom I had so desperately been searching for. Janis Joplin sang, "Freedom's just another word for nothing left to lose." Boy was she right! I went straight from my own childhood into raising my own children. I continued to go to school though. That was such a priority! Getting my high school diploma meant everything to me, as I had heard throughout my childhood that without it, I would be nothing. And I wasn't going to be nothing! I already felt like a weirdo! So, after being married for two years, in June of 1976, I did indeed graduate with my class as well as with honors. My firstborn son was at my graduation, and I was seven months pregnant with my second child. Funny how *those* things were accepted in the seventies. Becoming a mother while you are still a child was OK, but talking to Angels and the other side was weird? Something to ponder later on, I suppose. Not now—but later. Like much later. OK—like never! Who cares?

I knew by the time I was in my mid-twenties that I would have to do something about *this gift*. I could always feel not only Angels but also the dead now pushing me to share information. And I had another problem brewing, not like I needed one more! I couldn't tell the difference between Angels from the dead sometimes. Everything got all tangled up.

So—*How* became the question. How in the name of God was I supposed to do this?

Well, I surely didn't know *how and when*, but I knew with all of my very being that I was to be a healer of the heart and the mind. And my unseen friends were beginning to push quite forcefully. And I'm not real sure, but pretty sure, that this is known as a calling. Well that was just great! I had a calling! However, the million-dollar question still remained. What in the heck was I supposed to do with it?

Chapter Six

Stranger Encounter

Frank: Eat Your Lasagna!

My very first encounter with a "stranger reading," meaning someone I did not know, happened in my late twenties. As I think back on it now, and as I have thought back on this incident throughout the years, I truly do wonder why I didn't pursue this spiritual adventure in my life sooner. I suppose the timing wasn't right or I would have. I simply wasn't ready. Still trying to avoid that rejection, I guess. It's just that plain and simple. The year was 1985.

> Average cost of new house $89,330
> Median price of an existing home $75,500
> Average income per year $22,100
> Average monthly rent $375
> Average price for new car $9,005
> 1 gallon of gas $1.09
> Movie ticket $2.75
> US postage stamp 22 cents
> Bacon per pound $1.65

A joint American-French expedition located the wreck of the *Titanic*.

President Reagan announced Strategic Defense Weapons (SDI) will not impact arms talks.

US

The Unabomber killed his first victim.

New York Stock Exchange closed for the day for Hurricane Gloria.

Life insurance companies began screening for AIDs, causing an outcry by civil liberties groups.

And—nowhere in the events of history reported for that year did anyone ever mention that my gift would include my first real reading!

I was at the grocery store with my two eldest boys who were nine and ten years old at the time, and I had my hands full. Raising those two boys almost killed me! They were quite a handful; running all over the store, knocking things over, and terrorizing the supermarket. They were unruly and had no discipline! Who in the heck was their mother anyway? Oh yeah, that would be me. But I was young when I had them, they were only fourteen months apart, and I had no idea how to raise children. I always knew what NOT to do, but when it came down to knowing what *to* do, I had no clue! So, I had two heathens with me that day, and I grabbed what I needed very quickly and headed for the checkout line, scolding both of them under my breath through clenched teeth every step of the way.

As I stood waiting in line, begging my boys to behave—while at the same time allowing them to grab candy bars—I felt a presence to my right. I truly thought to myself, oh no, another nosy body who is going to tell me that my children are out of control and how I should parent them. Not today, I thought, please. But as I turned around to look, no one was there. I could clearly feel someone standing there but no one was there! And that is when a thought came to me that wasn't my own. It was a woman and she said, "That is how he eats now that I am gone."

I immediately looked around, hoping upon all hopes in the world that first of all, no one was looking at me, and second of all, that perhaps someone was indeed talking to me from the other side of the snack shelf that adorns every line in a grocery store. No possible luck!

Who was that, I thought? Or better yet, *what* was that?

I looked to see a little old man standing ahead of me in line as the cashier was scanning what few items he had in front of him. I peeked around the counter on her side so I could see what was on the conveyor belt and there was nothing. His few items were in front of him ready to be bagged and the cashier was saying something to him.

"How are you doing, Frank?" she asked sympathetically.

"Oh, I'm making do," he said, as I noticed a few cans of soup, a can of tuna, and a loaf of bread being placed in his little plastic sack. He was a cute little fella. The kind of guy you would like to talk to. The type of guy you'd find gardening in his yard on a Sunday afternoon.

Again, the thought came to me. "That is how he eats, see," she said. "He loves lasagna, it was his favorite. I made it for him all the time, and he will never eat it again. Please," the thought begged me, "you must ask him to eat better. Please tell him to buy some lasagna or have someone make it for him."

I felt as though I were frozen in time, as though time in that grocery store had stopped abruptly and completely. I swear had I looked at a clock at that very moment, the hands would not have turned. Everything around me went completely silent and I could feel her love for him.

He grabbed his bag and headed out of the store waving his hand behind and over his head at the cashier as she asked him to take care.

I stepped up to the register and paid for my groceries, not even thinking about my boys and where they were. And—astonishingly, they were right beside me and they were, well, behaving. Just standing to my left, and they were behaving like little gentlemen.

I took my own few items in my own plastic bag, thanking the cashier as I headed for the exit door, telling the boys to follow Momma; we were going home. Or—perhaps I should drop you both off with a babysitter and Momma will studiously check herself into the nut house! Yes, that is what I thought because that is exactly how I felt.

What an imagination! I should pursue my writing career as a novelist! I could write fiction books for little kids who would buy this crap I was peddling!

As I exited the store, I stopped dead in my tracks. There stood little old Frank. He seemed to be waiting for a ride, as his gaze was fixated across the parking lot.

She was really pushing on me now. It felt as though she may just run right up my backside. Like when we were kids and someone would come up from behind us and give us that notorious and irritating flat tire and crunch the back of our sneaker right off the back of our heel.

Please tell him she was urging, please!

I had no clue who *she*, even was, and I don't think it mattered to me. What mattered was the emotion I felt. I had to help her. Not *him*—but *her*! I had to tell Frank to eat lasagna for heaven's sake! I had to!

So, before I even gave myself time to stop and think about what I was about to do, I walked up to that little old man, and I spoke the words that were somehow coming out of my mouth before I could even reason what I was about to say.

"Excuse me," I pardoned myself as I walked up to him.

He turned to look at me through old, tired eyes that were very kind and searching. I felt him, and I felt his loneliness. I felt her and her love and compassion, and I realized I was in the middle of the two of them. I was—in—the—middle!

Mid·dle
1. *equally distant from the extremes or outer limits; central: the middle point of a line; the middle singer in a trio.*
2. *intermediate or intervening: the middle distance.*
3. *medium or average: a man of middle size.*

noun
The point, part, position, etc., equidistant from extremes or limits. something intermediate; mean.
(in farming) the ground between two rows of plants.

Synonyms
1. ***equidistant, halfway, medial, midway. midpoint. Middle, center, midst indicate something from which two or more other things are (approximately or exactly) equally distant. Middle denotes, literally or figuratively, the point or part equidistant from or intermediate between extremes or limits in space or in time: the middle of a road. Center, a more precise word, is ordinarily applied to a point within circular, globular, or regular bodies, or wherever a similar exactness appears to exist: the center of the earth; it may also be used metaphorically (still suggesting the core of a sphere): center of interest. Midst usually suggests that a person or thing is closely surrounded or encompassed on all sides, especially by that which is thick or dense: the midst of a storm.***

"Frank, is it?" I asked politely.

Now his look turned to wonderment.

"I overheard the clerk," I explained.

"Oh," he chuckled, clearly relieved, "Can I help you, miss?" he asked.

"Well," I began, "please don't be afraid of me or think I'm a freak, because I'm not." I tried to convince him, although I truly felt like one.

He simply stood there staring into my eyes with a question in his.

"Your wife," I began. "She wants you to eat better. She says your favorite dish was lasagna, not just any lasagna but *her* lasagna, and you loved it. She wants you to go get some, somewhere. She loves you, Frank, and she knows you are lonely. She knows you miss her desperately, but she is so much better now. No more tubes, Frank. No more pain. Please go get some lasagna," I said. "Please try to eat better."

And that was it. I wasn't sure of everything I had just said; it came out so fast it was like I didn't even have time to think to speak.

We both just stood there for another frozen moment in time. His eyes were searching mine, accompanied by a squint before he reached out and he touched the underside of my arm, and he hazily asked, "Who are you?"

"My name is Marti," I answered him. "Marti Tote." And then I followed that sentence with an apology. "I'm sorry," I said, more speaking to the sidewalk than I was to him. And I *was* sorry. I was sorry that I was Marti Tote and that I had the ability to do what I had just indeed done. I didn't want to see that look in his eyes. The look I had always dreaded coming back at me. The look that said, you are a freak!

"How do you know?" he asked very methodically. "How could you know that?" he added with emphasis.

"I don't know," I said.

"Are you gifted?" he asked.

"I don't know," I said again, still just a bit dazed and confused.

"No," he said. "You are! You must be a medium," he added.

Oh. Snap! There it was! That word! The one that makes everyone freak out!

"No," I stammered, "I don't think so."

Still touching my arm, he very tenderly—as though he were comforting me—said, "You do, you have a gift. Thank you. Thank you whoever you are, whatever you want to call yourself, thank you! No one could have known that. Not about the lasagna—but the tubes. All the tubes she was connected to."

Holy heck! I had forgotten about that slight comment, that one minute detail. It wasn't the lasagna at all. It was the fact that she had told me that she had been hooked up to tubes! It was her way of telling him it was really her! She had no intentions of telling him to eat right at all! She just needed to tell him that she was OK. And that she loved him. I had been duped by a dead person!

So what did I do? Well, I will tell you. Nothing! Not a gosh darn stinking thing.

I simply turned, gathered up my very well-mannered boys, and I walked away.

"Thank you," he continued hollering at me over and over again as I walked away.

"Thank you!"

I don't know why that incident scared me so badly. I never told anyone. I was amazed, although I still doubted myself, even though I had said something to that man that I could not possibly have known. And it still amazes me to this day every time I deliver a message. And yes, I do still doubt myself in every reading I convey. To this day, I still wonder how I can be such a great guesser. And I get more excited than the client sitting in my room. Because to me, it is a miracle! And it always will be! Thank God!

Chapter Seven

Arrival

They're Heeeere!

Shortly after what happened in the last chapter occurred, my first *adult* encounter with an Angel happened when my only daughter was about three years old. I was thirty years old and I myself didn't actually see the Angel; *she* did! The year was 1988.

Average cost of new house $91,600.00
Average income per year $24,450
Average monthly rent $420
Average price for new car $10,400
One gallon of gas 91 cents
Movie ticket $3.50
US postage stamp 24 cents
Dozen eggs 65 cents

First transatlantic fiber optic cable was laid able to carry forty thousand telephone calls simultaneously.
Stephen Hawking published A Brief History of Time.
The first major computer virus infected computers connected to the Internet.
The Hubble Space Telescope was put into operation.
The US stealth bomber was unveiled.

Using carbon dating, it was established that the Turin Shroud cannot be the burial cloth of Christ.

The antidepressant Prozac was introduced, quickly becoming the market leader for treating depression.

First use of laser eye surgery in the United States.

Over one-third of Yellowstone National Park was destroyed when a series of more than 250 small fires combined with the 1988 drought to destroy 793,880 acres of the park.

US shuttle program resumed two and half years after the Challenger disaster.

And—nowhere in the events of history reported for that year did anyone ever mention that Angels were indeed right here on this earth!

When I became pregnant with my fourth child, I came to the brilliant realization that I would not be able to work and afford daycare. My two youngest children would not yet be in school; therefore, I would be working only to cover the daycare expenses. Being the ever so innovative genius that I had truly become—as well as the daughter of a very hard-working janitor who did not believe in welfare unless you truly *couldn't* work—I decided to get a license to do daycare in my home. This way, I could have my children at home, be there for the older ones when they came home from school, and make a living all at the same time. Not to mention that I just so happened to love children. Problem solved!

I lived in a tri-level home at the time and had converted the entire downstairs family room into a playroom. It was whimsical and very accommodating. There was a bathroom on that floor as well as another bedroom, which was great for nap time. The garage was off the laundry room, also on the same floor. It was like a little apartment within a house.

Each afternoon, after I fed the children lunch and laid them down for their naps, I would vacuum and do cleanup while they were lying in their cribs and on their mats getting sleepy. I think the hum of the vacuum helped to lull them to sleep.

On one particular afternoon, I had taken my three-year-old daughter upstairs to her bedroom where she took her nap—mostly because she always kept the other children awake—and I tucked her in as usual and then went back downstairs to begin my afternoon ritual. As I was vacuuming and cleaning up, I had no clue she had slipped out the garage door somehow without my seeing her and gone out to the dog run where we had two full-grown boxers.

As I was running the vacuum I had this incredible urge to check on her. *Go check on Jessica!* However, I shrugged it off and continued on with my chores. Then it happened again but this time it was a clear and very precise message to *GO CHECK ON JESSICA!*

Irritated by this thing—this knowing—that would happen from time to time and wouldn't stop until I acted on it, I shut off the vacuum cleaner and headed upstairs to take a quick peek into her bedroom and to my absolute horror, she was gone! I checked all three of the upstairs bedrooms and both bathrooms before I raced down the stairs screaming her name as absolute and undeniable panic consumed me. I was frantic and I searched everywhere but she was nowhere to be found!

I raced back downstairs to the playroom and headed for the garage but before I even got to the laundry room, the garage door opened and there she stood, crying! She was filthy and disheveled and her neck clearly had a horrible bruise directly above her collarbone! I slid to my knees and began wiping her hair from her eyes, smearing tears and dirt all over her face as I asked her through my own tears of relief, where she had been.

She explained to me that she had heard our dogs barking, and she thought they needed her so she went out to the dog run. But when she did, Cowboy, our male boxer, who we always kept chained because he was a jumper and a runner, was very excited to see her and he knocked her down. In all his excitement, he got his chain wrapped around her neck and she was being dragged all over the dog run and couldn't breathe!

I was astounded. Trying to process all I was hearing as I tried to calm my little girl, and in the midst of my own shock and disbelief, all I could think of to ask was how in the world she got out of there. Her answer to me was quite straight and to the point.

"The man came down from the top of the fence, and he unhooked the chain from my neck."

OK, now I was truly confused. There had been a man in the dog run with my daughter!

"What man?" I asked.

"God," she said quite frankly. "And he had wings, Mommy, just like you said! He made the dogs lay down and he lifted me up into his arms and carried me into the garage and opened the door so I could come in."

I immediately told her to stay put and I walked out the garage door from the laundry room, went through the garage and out to the dog run, all the while frantically searching the garage for an intruder.

Both of our boxers were lying down and calm, not even jumping up to come and greet me. I stood there scanning the dog run as though I would perhaps find a man out there. And that is when I knew. I felt that so familiar presence that had always surrounded me. The dogs were still calm and lying down as I turned to go back into the house. They never even lifted their heads to acknowledge me.

I came back into the house and took Jessica into the tiny bathroom off the playroom, and I began to clean her up, noticing that her bruise wasn't quite as bad as it had been when I first saw her. I undressed her to check for other injuries. Her back and legs had a few scratches but that was it. Then the doorbell rang.

Great, I thought, probably a parent coming to pick up a child early, and mine looks like she had just been smacked around!

I scooped up Jessica, placed her on my hip, and walked up the stairs to the main floor. I set her down on a kitchen chair, telling her to stay put while I got the door. The doorbell rang again.

I opened the front door and there stood a woman in a jogging outfit, headband and all, clearly bending down to catch her breath. She stood up as I opened the door, and through her winded voice she told me she had been taking her daily run and she just had to turn around and come back to make sure the little kid she heard screaming from my backyard was OK.

"You heard her screaming?" I asked, clearly astonished.

A Whisper in the Wings

"Yes, I did," she said, "but I knew her dad or…" she shrugged her shoulders, "whomever, had come out to get her."

She must have thought I was crazy because the next thing out of my mouth was, "Did you see him?"

She hesitated and then said no, she didn't. She just saw through the slats in the fence from the sidewalk that someone had come to her rescue. And then we both simply stood there looking at each other in very uncomfortable silence before I found my voice and thanked her for checking up on her. Then I simply explained to her what had happened, leaving the part out about *who* or *what* had rescued her and she left. I wondered if she had been real. For a split second I wondered if *anything* was real.

I knew in my heart of hearts and my knowing of knowings that there simply had to be a logical explanation for what had happened to my daughter that afternoon and there was. Yes, there absolutely was! An Angel had rescued my daughter from a horrible accident. I know it wasn't her time to go, or they would not have intervened. They were trying to get my attention and they knew I would believe my child before I would believe myself! And well, they surely succeeded!

Jessica barely remembers that incident but she remembers enough to recite the parts that perplex her. I never asked her, nor did I tell her that story as she got older. I waited until she brought it up, and then I would ask the same questions. What did the man look like and what did he do? She gave me the same answer every time I asked throughout the years. He had wings and he was on the fence and he came down from the fence, picked her up into his arms, gently unwrapping the dog chain from her neck and then carried her through the garage to the door that led into the house. She does not remember what his face looked like, nor does she remember what he was wearing.

My daughter is now twenty-eight years old with a child of her own, and she is a very gifted healer with her hands. She can heal the body, and she can feel when there are things that don't belong there. That began around the time she turned ten. So the question is, was she saved that day to help others? Did that rescuing Angel grace her with a gift that day so that she could give back? Well I'm not a real good guesser, never have been, so I will leave that question up to you to answer for yourselves. Coincidence, Divine Intervention, or perhaps just a little girl's wild imagination? What do you believe?

Chapter Eight

My Awakening

And I Never Even Set My Alarm!

I titled this chapter my awakening because well, I sort of muddled through the next few years until I had an awakening—therefore, appropriately titled. I was thirty-four years old. The year was 1992.

Average cost of new house $122,500
Average income per year $30,030
Average monthly rent $519
Cost of a gallon of gas $1.05
One pound of bacon $1.92
Average cost of new car $16,950.00

United States presidential election, Bill Clinton (Democrat) defeated George H. W. Bush (Republican) and Ross Perot (no party).
Microsoft released Windows 3.1.
Microsoft released Microsoft Works.
AT&T released a video telephone for $1,499.
The first nicotine patch was introduced to help people stop smoking.
Space Shuttle Endeavor had a successful maiden voyage.

> **And nowhere in the events of history reported for that year did anyone ever mention that I lost my most cherished childhood friend. My buddy—My everything—My dad.**

The year, 1992, was a tough year for me. Actually tough is putting it mildly. We have all heard of hell week. Well, for me it was hell year! My president lost the election. My ball team lost the World Series. And I lost my dad!

My father was diagnosed with terminal cancer that year so I, being the ever so gallant daughter that I was, ventured off to Southern California to stay with him until he died. In all actuality, I truly went there thinking I could stop fate, but that is another book all together. A book that some of you have already read.

Taking care of my father during his final days here on this earth must have been in the plan for me (DUH), because it was during that time at his home when I just couldn't ignore what was happening to me any longer. Lovely! Just lovely!

I was devastated to learn of my father's diagnosis, and denial took on a whole new meaning for me that year. I absolutely was not going to lose my dad! There had to be something that *someone, somewhere* could do! However, there was truly nothing left that could be done. And I eventually had to face that horrible fact. My dad had cancer throughout his entire body, most likely originating from the breast or a mole on the breast. So we will never know if was melanoma or breast cancer, and I guess it doesn't really matter now anyway. What matters is what happened and what I was graced with to observe while I was there. That is, after all, the very reason I ended up there in the first place. Of course I didn't know that then. Ah, but *they* did!

My dad saw and heard folks who had come to help him cross over. You know, so he wouldn't be alone. We are all graced with that divine service when we leave this place, by the way. I'm letting you know just in case you all might have been wondering. Well, at the time, I had no clue but I'm a really fast learner and it's a darn good thing because this was the year that *they* decided to really get my attention, and that, they truly did!

When my dad asked me if I heard them, I lied and said no. When he asked me if I felt them, I lied and said no. When he asked me if I saw them, I said no, but I didn't lie about that. I truly did not see a thing. Well, sort of.

There were a couple of times when I did see, well, something out of the corner of my eye while I sat in his tiny living room waiting for him to emerge from his bedroom during his naps. It was getting very close to his departure. However, I had no way of knowing that at the time. And I have to admit that I saw two of them face-to-face and not out of the corner of my eye! And let me tell you, whoever they were, well, they scared the living daylights outa' me!

One was a tall man figure. He had to be over seven feet tall and although I could not see his facial features I could clearly see his size and his squared shoulders. He was a dark fuzzy energy and he didn't actually walk but he more like hovered very quickly from my dad's bedroom to the bathroom. I did get up to investigate, thinking my dad had wandered into the bathroom, only to discover that he was sound asleep in bed. Funny how our minds want so badly to explain the unexplainable, isn't it? I mean, my dad certainly wasn't seven feet tall and he hadn't moved that fast in years! And yet, there I stood, trying my hardest to make sense out of what I was seeing. Waiting as though perhaps a cue card would fall from the ceiling with the answer! But it didn't. No, it surely did not. I didn't move one muscle and neither did he—or it—or—whatever. I was petrified with fear, and yet I didn't scream, nor did I want to. I simply stood there trying to find answers to questions to which there were no logical explanations for whatsoever at all! And then it/he simply vanished, and I simply did not. I asked in my mind—who are you? However, sadly, I received no answer.

The next incident was a woman figure, much smaller in stature, and she simply stood in the hallway as if she were waiting for me to follow her. She too was a fuzzy energy but I could clearly see that she was wearing a long flowing dress. Again I got up to investigate, but unlike her friend, she didn't move when I walked toward her. So I stopped and just stood there staring at her. And once again, my mind was trying to make sense of what I was seeing but to no avail. I knew in my heart what I was seeing. She was clearly a nurturer. Of this I was positive! And I wasn't as afraid of her as I was of the larger one. Perhaps it was the size? Again in my mind I asked, who are you? And this time I clearly received an answer. You know who I am! Well, uh, no, I didn't, but yet again, I did. I knew she was an Angel. And I knew she was an escort. And I felt very sleepy and at peace. And with a caring feeling that only an Angel can leave you with, she vanished. Just like that! And my only regret is that I wish now that I had told my dad. But I was much too afraid at that time in my life to admit such things. I simply wasn't ready, AGAIN!

When I would sit with my dad as he slept, I could hear their thoughts in that bedroom. I could hear so many conversations going on all at once that it sounded, at times, as though I were in a crowded ballroom but even with all the noise, It was peaceful in that bedroom. I felt safe and good in there. At the time, I never even stopped to wonder why or what was happening to me. I simply sat in there and felt as though they embraced me. It felt like home. Yes! That was it! I was home again!

After my father's death, I had to of course eventually go home, to my earthly home. And as I left what used to be my father's home, I felt so very empty and lonely. Like the day I left Tommy behind. However, something very different happened to me this time. They came with me! And so did my dad!

I couldn't connect to my dad's thoughts like I could theirs, but I felt him. I felt him around me all the time. I grieved over my father's death for many years. And I dreamed about him. And that is when I became fascinated with dreams as well, as I became aware that if we dream of the dead, they don't come to us, but we go to them! And please, don't ask me to explain, because I simply can't. I just know it to be true. Once again, my book, my knowing! They are compliments of none other than my friends on the other side.

Some of the dreams were silly and scary but some were so real that I knew I was actually seeing and communicating with my dad. In one dream in particular, we were standing in a huge library. He was holding a large stack of papers, and although his lips were not moving, he was saying to me, "Go ahead, dear, this is the stuff dreams are made of!" as he was shoving this large stack of paper toward me, wanting me to take it from him. I looked at it and there were words on the paper that I could see but I couldn't read them. It wasn't until years later, when I printed out my first manuscript of my father's story, and I was holding it in my hands, that I remembered that dream! I dropped my entire manuscript! It is one of those moments in my life when my stomach seized and I couldn't have moved my feet had my butt been on fire! I believe my dad wanted me to write that book. His story. He knew it would help others, and it has.

I also remember the very last dream I had of my father during that time in my life. We were standing in this beautiful entryway with white cloudy walls and a huge door that stood far higher than I could see. He was saying good-bye. I was crying, and he was reassuring me that I would be OK. I was pleading with him not to go, but he was telling me it was time.

When I awoke, I was in a panic, but I clearly remember sucking in air as though I hadn't been breathing. I felt as though, well, that I was coming back from somewhere. That is the most honest way I can explain it. I was very sad and the tears on my face were real. I got out of bed still sobbing uncontrollably, and just like we see people do in the movies, I ran to the bathroom and got real close to the mirror, and I touched my own face. I didn't know where I was but there wasn't a doubt in my mind as to where I had been.

That dream came five years after my father's death. And I didn't dream of him until many years later. About six months ago to be exact, and I think he simply wanted to check in with me.

We were walking down a long arched, stark white tunnel side by side, holding hands and it opened up into the most beautiful long country road I have ever seen. The road was adorned on both sides with white three-rail fences, and there were beautiful green pastures as far as the eye could see. Huge trees were standing about every twenty feet or so along those fences and all my horses that had crossed over were grazing in the pastures. My dad was telling me that this was heaven—*my heaven*! And when I turned to kiss his cheek, he was gone, and I woke up. In every dream I have ever had of my dad, every time I try to kiss his wrinkly cheek, just to feel and smell him again, he is gone. And if you don't mind my saying so, gosh darn that ticks me off to no avail!

Yes, all these things I speak of are true. And it is very difficult for me to expose such sacred, private and personal happenings with others. I feel rather—well, exposed! However, I have to share the truth with you. I must be honest and forthright so that perhaps someone who may be looking for answers can have a starting point. That is—after all, why I had to write this story. For you! My many gifted friends. And we *are all* gifted! There are just so many facets of gifted that all we have to do is find the one where we best fit in. Sure makes it a whole lot easier when you think of it that way now, doesn't it?

Yes, 1992 will always be the year that will never leave my memory. I came home with a knowing that I simply could no longer ignore, and I'm pretty sure I didn't want to anymore. Can't really remember that too clearly but I'm pretty sure. I think that once we experience death up close and personal—well, lots of things change, and I know from talking to many other folks about this subject, we all ask the same question of our deceased loved ones. Whether spoken out loud or said as a soft whisper, or perhaps just in our minds: *"Where are you?"*

Chapter Nine

All Right Already! I Get It!

Sort of…

After the death of my father, the good old proverbial crystal ball really began to roll and certainly not by my choice, I might add. It was as though someone opened the flood gates of communication from the other side to here! Huh, wait a minute. Wouldn't that be the gates of heaven? Perhaps. Although I believe that everyone's heaven is different. We all get to pick our own, you know. Yep, just gather up all the most wonderful things you love and adore with all your heart and soul, from rainy days to PBJs and create your own heaven! I learned that little piece of valuable information through absolute and undeniable experience from of all my friends who have crossed over. Good to have such knowledgeable friends hanging around, don't you think? Well, I'm not so sure I was ready, but here they came! And they came hard and fast.

I began to research what I had been experiencing all my life. I went to the library and checked out every book I could find on any subject that seemed to fit. Some helped and some confused me, but everything led me right to where I am.

In 1998, or somewhere around that time, I bought my very first laptop computer. This opened up an entire new world for me. I sat for hours researching and learning. One search term led me to another and then another. Some things locked into place like a missing puzzle piece and some didn't. For instance, I knew beyond a shadow of a doubt that I *was not* a premonition person. On the other hand, I learned beyond another shadow of a doubt that I *was* definitely a medium, and that I was absolutely clairvoyant. Both terms frightened me in that I just couldn't bring myself to share those facts with anyone. I hated the word psychic. It made me feel like a freak (again). So just exactly what was I to call myself, because normal, whatever normal is, just wasn't it either!

I gained a lot of insight and was given years packed full of signs and absolute and undeniable gifts! I was forty-three years old when the next wave hit. The year was 2001.

Average cost of new house $136,150
Average median income $42,350
Average monthly rent $715
Cost of a gallon of gas $1.46
Average cost of new car $25,850
US postage stamp 34 cents
One pound of bacon $3.22
Ground coffee per pound $3.06
Loaf of bread $1.82
Dozen eggs 90 cents

Known simply as 9/11. On September 11, 2001, nineteen hijackers simultaneously took control of four US domestic commercial airliners. The hijackers crashed two planes into the World Trade Center in New York City, one into each of the two tall towers. Within two hours, both towers collapsed. The hijackers crashed the third aircraft into the US Department of Defense headquarters, the Pentagon, in Arlington County, Virginia. The fourth plane crashed into a rural field in Somerset County, Pennsylvania, following apparent passenger resistance.

Timothy James McVeigh was executed for the Oklahoma City bombing.

It was the "Summer of the Shark," so named after a number of shark attack fatalities.

Enron filed for Chapter Eleven bankruptcy protection.

A series of anthrax attacks spread fear among the American public, and several people were infected by handling infected letters.

Richard C. Reid, dubbed by the press as the shoe bomber, attempted to blow up an American Airlines plane.

And – nowhere in the events of history reported for that year did anyone ever mention that my life would change forever, and there was no looking back!

The year 2001 was quite a year for me. I believe it was for all us actually. After 9/11, I feel it safe to say that sadly, I don't think *anyone* was ever the same again.

We bought our very first house in the country so I didn't have to board my horse anymore. I owned my own temporary staffing service, and business was great. I got up every morning, saddled my horse, took my dog, went for a ride, came home, showered, and went to work. Then I came home every night, saddled my horse, took my dog, and went for another ride. Came home, fed my horse and retired for the evening with a good book. My youngest child, my daughter, was now sixteen and I was finally living the life that I had always dreamed of. Life was perfect! Huh boy!

The summer before the 9/11 attack, I had become very close with my daughter-in-law Lindy. She is married to my second-eldest son, Michael. She was actually the first person—other than my sister Jodie—I ever told there might be something going on with me. She was skeptical but open-minded and I was—well—skeptical!

I believe it was actually the year before, give or take a few months, that I had been home early one day and just happened to catch Oprah's afternoon show. Her guest that day was a woman by the name of Doreen Virtue. I was very taken by her. I had seen other psychics on television but there was something different about this one. She talked about Angels! And she truly looked like one to me. I was mesmerized by what she was saying. After the show, I had to call Lindy at once to tell her all about this Doreen Virtue person!

Shortly thereafter, and I can't recall exact timeframes, but it had to be mere weeks later, Lindy called me and told me that the woman I had seen on Oprah was coming to Reno, and we should try to go see her. Maybe she will read you, Lindy was saying. Read me? What a concept! I had never even thought of having someone read me. So we found out the time and the place, and we were going to have to get there a little late because of our work schedules, but we decided that we could go anyway.

On our way there, I was as nervous as a cat on a hot tin roof. I don't know why to this day—but I was scared. And all I kept saying on our way downtown was, she just has to see me. She doesn't even have to talk to me—she just has to see me. She just has to see…

We arrived late as anticipated and the place was packed. We had to stand all the way in the back by all these tables that were set up with beautiful decks of cards and books. I had never in my life held a deck of tarot cards, but these were Angel cards. Angel cards? I had no clue what those were, but as she began to wrap up her seminar, she said she would stay for signings of her books and cards. So I told Lindy to grab a deck of those mysterious Angel cards and we would have her sign them. I knew nothing of her books, and I didn't have time to browse! I was on a mission, and I was afraid that if we didn't hurry, we wouldn't have a chance to get in line. However, to my astonishment, by the time we got through the line and paid for the cards, there wasn't a soul in line and she was sitting on the stairs that led up to the stage. Just sitting there reading something! So as we began our journey up the main aisle toward her, I was certain that security would stop us and tell us it was too late to have anything signed. But they didn't. No one said a word to us.

We got about ten feet away from her when all a sudden, she looked up from what she was reading, looked right at me, and said, "I see you." Just as calmly as one might say, I'm hungry.

I was so shocked by what she had just said to me that all I could think of to do was to thrust the cards toward her, asking her, "Will you sign my cards?" Brilliant! Just brilliant!

She stood up and extended her arm to take the deck of cards from me and as she did, she asked me a question. "Why are you so afraid of what you are hearing? You can hear Angels as well as those who have crossed over. They are all around you," she added.

I was dumbfounded! Finally! An answer! Confirmation! Validation! Oh just great! So what did that mean?

I gave her the RCA dog cock of my head before I simply stepped forward and hugged her. And she hugged me back, whispering in my ear that I was a little light worker. "Nothing to be afraid of," she added.

Uh huh, well, I had never heard that term before, and quite frankly—it fit! The final puzzle piece had been locked into place by this Angel-hearing person and she felt like an Angel! She was so peaceful and serene and I could feel her. And I could feel and hear *her* Angels and they were happy. And I knew! I'm not sure how I knew but I knew that this meeting had been planned long ago. Long before she or I had ever breathed air in this place. Time seemed to stand completely still—again.

As I was leaving, which wasn't easy, I turned back around, and I asked her, "But how do I know if they are Angels or people who have crossed over?"

She simply smiled that Angelic smile of hers and said, "That's easy. Ask them *how* they crossed over. Those who have crossed over from this place always know how they left. Our Angels were born with us. They have never been in an earthly body. They have never died. If they answer you, they have crossed over." And that was it! That was my "ah ha!" moment of all moments! How simple life had just become! Well—sort of.

"Now I don't want to confuse anyone, as I'm not saying our deceased loved ones cannot watch over us, because of course they can; and they do! However, it has been my experience that our Angels are more apt to be earthbound and the ones to intervene if need be. They have absolutely no problem showing up as *anyone* or *anything*, for that matter. Angels are amazing beings! And they are busy! Very, very busy indeed! After all, they are the keepers of divine timing!

After the meeting with that earth Angel who called herself Doreen Virtue, I went home and opened my very first deck of Angel cards. I read the instructions, and I did exactly what they said. "Healing with the Angels," was my very first deck of Angel cards. Now I own them all, along with every book she has ever written, although it is tough to keep up with that Angelic person.

I was very selfish with my new deck of cards and I didn't want anyone else to touch them! I was so afraid they would become tainted!

I called Lindy that night, and I swore to her that the darn things were magic! And I just knew they were because that Angelic lady touched *my* deck of cards! And they sit in my session's room to this day. And I still don't let anyone touch them. They are very special to me.

A few months later, we went over to Mike and Lindy's house for dinner. Lindy has a large family, so some of her cousins were there as well as her friends. I was sitting in the living room among everyone, eating my dinner, just minding my own business, when all a sudden I got a clear and precise message that there was new life beginning in that room. New life? What in the heck did that mean? New life? Oh! Someone was pregnant! I was shocked as I looked around wondering who. So I got up and walked into the kitchen. I whispered to Lindy that someone in her house was pregnant.

"Really?" she said as she raised her eyebrows and looked out into the living room. "Who is it?" she whispered back to me.

"I don't know," I said, "but I know that what I am hearing is strong and correct."

So we pondered and wondered secretly. That was about the end of it until I got home that night, and she called me.

"Could it be me?" she asked.

I was blindsided by the question. "I don't know," I said. "Do you feel pregnant?"

"I don't know," she said. "I've never been pregnant before."

I was so excited in that if it *was* her, I was going to be a grandmother! So my mind was going in one direction and hers was going in another. It always did, always has, and for this I am very thankful!

Then, just as though it was a normal thing to say, she said, "Grab your Angel cards and ask the Angels for an answer."

Huh, what a concept! So I grabbed my Angel cards and I closed my bedroom door and sat cross-legged on my bed. I opened the box and carefully shuffled my cards ever so gingerly, and then I asked, "Top, bottom, or middle?"

"Middle," she said.

I drew the middle card and it said children!

I almost screamed into the phone, and I hadn't even read the card meaning yet.

"Put it back," she insisted, "and draw again."

"OK," I said and placed it back in the middle of the deck. Once again I shuffled my Angel cards ever so carefully and asked her top, bottom, or middle?

"Top," she said.

So I drew the top card and the children card came up again!

I was absolutely and undeniably shocked!

"You are pregnant!" I said.

That was my very first card reading, and she *was* pregnant!

Lindy not only became my best friend that year, but she also volunteered herself to be my guinea pig. We spoke on the phone every morning and I would listen to her Angels and tell her things that were going on in her life. She had agreed not to share things with me to see how accurate I was. And accurate doesn't even touch what happened to me that year! No, because sadly, I also realized that year that I could actually draw from the person I was reading and read the person that they loved or were concerned about. I say sadly, because I also realized I could receive messages about health. I could see the inside of the body and I could feel what was happening. I have learned that too was an amazing gift. Had I not been able to do this, Lindy would not have taken the opportunity to go to her papa and have one last, very meaningful conversation with him, as one morning while talking to her on the phone, she asked me to look at her papa's health. And when I did, I saw some sort of a starburst in his stomach area.

"What does that mean?" she asked.

"I don't know," I said. And I didn't know. I had no clue what I was seeing or why. I had no clue about the human body in terms of organs or anything at all, for that matter. But one thing was for sure, I knew her papa had an aneurism in his stomach, and it was about to burst! I had no clue that people could even get an aneurism in their stomach. And neither did she, for that matter. Her papa had indeed been diagnosed with prostate cancer, but this was most peculiar to me. The stomach was a long way from the prostate. I was confused. And Lindy was confused as well but she trusted her Angels and heeded their advice when I told her that she didn't have much time left with him. She took advantage of that information and arranged a talk with her papa to tell him what he meant to her.

During that talk, she asked him if he was having stomach pain, and he told her he was. And that talk was indeed the last heartfelt conversation that Lindy would have with her papa. He died in his sleep that following May. Whether it was from an aneurism that had burst in his stomach will have to remain a mystery. Some things are just better left unknown. Doesn't really matter once someone is gone anyway. They are no longer here and we can't get them back. And that is a sad fact of life that not even God *can* or *will* do anything about.

I wasn't sure on that horrible morning in May, as we all gathered at Lindy's grandparents' house, if I wanted this gift or not. But I suppose now, looking back on all the precious warnings I have been given over the years since then, that I am probably blessed. I don't always get those warnings before someone goes. Only *they* know. Why and how they give me insight on some people and not others, I may never know. I don't get to pick what I am told. I *have* learned, however, that if *they* give us a health warning, we are sometimes allowed to change it. So, getting a health warning on someone isn't always bad news. Of course, if we already know that someone is on the way out of here by way of a diagnosis, that's kind of a no-brainer. However, I am never told exactly when the person will leave. Some things are just not meant to be known. And I am perfectly fine with that! Absolutely, positively, undeniably FINE!

I have learned not to question what I am being told. I am simply a reporter. A messenger of sorts, I suppose. And we have all heard the saying: "Don't shoot the messenger!" No, I suppose not. However, sometimes, *this* messenger truly does understand why someone would *want* to shoot the messenger. Yes, sadly, as we are about to find out, I surely do know.

Chapter Ten

My First Reading

Why, Oh Why Didn't I Just Stick to Writing?

THIS CHAPTER WILL be a bit different, as it was still 2001. So the only timeline from here on out will be my own. You see, time stopped in the year 2001. It did for many of us. But as for me, well, there is no time on the other side and I began to frequent the other side quite a bit. As a matter of fact; **somewhere in the events of history reported for that year—someone should have mentioned that my life would never again be the same and that time would stand completely still never to matter to me again!**

Sadly, I lost a good friend over my very first *real* reading. And by *real* I mean someone other than Lindy—oh and of course, Frank! I didn't plan to do a reading. Just like I didn't ask my friend's murdered daughter to visit me in my shower. But she did. Welcome to my new life!

So many things happened to me during the year 2001 that it surely seems as though it was more like *two* entire years packed into one. Maybe even three but who's counting? Well, I mean besides me?

My very first *real* reading, as I call it, happened very unexpectedly and the way it happened was just as unexpected.

I was living my dream life in the country with my horses and dogs, as I shared with you earlier, and I had met a woman a couple years before who owned her own business, which I will not disclose in this story for confidential reasons. Nonetheless, I believe we had become pretty good friends and I needed her services now and again. She was a lovely sweet soul and I really liked her.

Well, we got to chatting one day and I had sensed a sadness deep inside this woman long before; however, I never read someone without permission so I never asked about that deep-seeded sadness. It was none of my business. That is, until one day as we sat chatting out in my front yard under the shade of a beautiful tree, she asked me if I had ever heard of a particular murder that had taken place in our town many years before. Well, of course I had heard of this murder because it was simply mortifying!

It was an awful story and it made me very sad. There had been a young girl abducted from a local establishment in our town and later found murdered—and that girl had been this woman's daughter! I couldn't believe it! Oh my gosh! The pain she must have suffered! It was incomprehensible to me! I felt so very sorry for her, especially having four children of my own! I could not even imagine the agony this woman must have experienced. But all I did that day was listen to her. I shared with her how that story had haunted me from the day the headlines broke. I comforted and consoled her all I could. We made a connection that day. And I busted it into a million pieces about two years later.

I hadn't lived in my country home for very long before I called her one morning and made an appointment for her services. After coming home, I had to take a shower and get to work. And just for the record, we did not talk about or even mention her daughter that day. For heaven's sake, why would we?

I got in the shower, and as I closed my eyes and put my head back to rinse my hair, I saw a girl's face. Now, one would think that I should have jumped out of that shower like my rear was on fire, getting tangled up in the shower curtain in the process, falling and hitting my head on the commode, never to regain consciousness again! But I didn't. No, I surely did not! Because when this happens to me I go to another place. A place where time stands completely still and I become very calm, almost nonexistent. A place of total peace and serenity.

I examined this face with my eyes closed and I could understand her thoughts. And then her face turned into a movie—a black-and-white movie. I saw a huge gravel pit and down in the valley of that gravel pit was a girl. She was running. I then saw a girl laying to the left, on her side. I saw a man's hand and a plaid sleeve. He was holding a shovel. He went to the trunk of an old car. I saw the car clearly. Even though I could only see it in black and white, I could feel the colors of everything. He reached into the trunk and put the shovel there. Nothing was happening in the right order. But I watched, and I was mesmerized. I also began to shake, as I could feel the fear in the atmosphere just as I could feel the colors. He picked up a rock and he threw it down into the gravel pit. It hit the young girl in the head, and she fell down. Everything was in slow motion. I was terrified. Then I looked to my left again and the girl was still lying there, motionless. I couldn't see his face but I clearly felt what he looked like. And then the thought of a message came to me from her. I understood her clearly.

How long had I been standing in the shower with my head under water rinsing my hair? I felt dizzy and confused. Robotically, I turned the water off and got out of the shower. I felt very calm, yet I was shaking. I held the towel up to my face, hugging myself. I was freezing. And then it hit me. I had to call my friend and deliver the message that had been given to me by her daughter. A particular message that had been a question in my friend's mind since her daughter's murder. I had to help her! Yes! That is exactly what I was going to do!

I got dressed that morning and the task of delivering that message became overwhelming! It consumed me. This had never happened to me before, well, besides Frank, and I didn't know what to do. How would I call my friend and tell her what I indeed needed to tell her? How would I explain *how I knew*!

Well, my friends, I just did. I picked up the phone and called her, beginning with the sentence, "I don't really understand what I am about to say to you, but I have to share something with you." And so I began.

During that conversation, she continued to ask how I could know that! Several times. "No one knew that but the police," she said to me!

But I held steadfast to the task at hand. I had no choice. Somehow I knew the feeling of panic wouldn't leave me until I threw up all the information. And then I delivered the message.

"You have gone to bed every night of your life since her death wondering if she was conscious when he killed her. You wondered if she was scared. The answer is no. She was unconscious and laying on the hillside before he murdered her. She was not afraid. And she wants you to help her brother. He blames himself. I have no clue why, and I don't need to know. I didn't even know you had a son! But you must tell him not to blame himself. He is in trouble and he hasn't been home in a long time. You have to call him and bring him home."

There was complete silence on the phone for what seemed like an eternity to me. And then, I heard a light moaning, crying, and then sobbing. I felt sleepy and relieved.

She shared with me through sporadic sobs that after the murder, her son had left home and gotten into heavy drugs. And yes, every night as she laid her head on her pillow, she would talk to her daughter in her mind and ask her, were you scared? Did you know?

I remained silent, consumed in her sadness.

When she finally spoke again she asked how long I had been doing this. How did I know these things? And she also shared with me that years ago, her daughter and son had played on the very site where my house had been built! They had lived just down the road.

I sat very quietly on the other end of the line. I didn't understand what had just happened and I didn't know why. I couldn't believe that it all really meant something. I was in total shock and denial. I must have guessed all of it! I made the whole thing up in my wild imagination. I must have! But then—how? How could I have reported those things so accurately? I didn't feel as great as one would think. I felt awful.

After we hung up that day we had just one more conversation. She had found her son and told him everything, and she felt that she could now begin to help *him* heal after all the years had passed. This made me happy. And then, she wouldn't return my calls. Time after time I tried to reach her and she just wouldn't return my calls. Sorrowfully, I never heard from her again. I was sad and confused. I felt empty and swore I would never do it again—whatever *it* was. But I did. I had to. Because I also learned that year the meaning of the word calling. And it was overpowering. I had been given a job to do here in this place, and I knew it just as surely as I knew my own name.

I was not angry with my friend. Somehow I just knew and understood. I now know that my place in her life was so that this happening would take place, and then I was to move on. I was brought into her life and she into mine for a reason. A purpose. Once that purpose had been fulfilled, there was no need for us to see each other again. Not here in this place anyway. And thus began my new life. A life graced with peace, serenity, and undeniable loneliness!

Chapter Eleven

Alone

Loneliness Should Be a Four-Letter Word!

After that fine morning in the shower, I did the unthinkable. I told my husband, Bob. I'm not real sure what in the heck compelled me to do such a thing or even *why*, for that matter, but if I had to guess, my guess would be that I probably wanted and *needed* to share it with someone other than Lindy, and all I have to say about that is, well, bad move, Mart, old gal!

We were both getting ready for work one morning, and I told him I had something I desperately needed to share with him. He was very kind and accommodating, and he listened, but I received no feedback. Nothing! Just a look on his face as though I had taken on the appearance of a chimpanzee standing before him! When I was finished explaining what must have sounded more like the telling of a movie than a true happening, I asked him what he thought. All he could say was, "I don't know, babe." Well of course he didn't know! How could he have possibly known or even understood something that I myself, the notorious *babe*, couldn't even understand, and it was happening to *me*!

Well, all I can say is the loneliness had begun. The feeling of being different was not an entirely new feeling for me, as we already know, but I actually felt once again, like a freak. And, I never brought it up to him again. Well, not for a few years anyway. I hid my Angel cards and took them out only when I was alone. I researched things on the Internet in private as well. I felt so very isolated. Sure, there were people all over the Internet and on television who were like me. But they were famous and I—was not!

So it was back to Lindy, and eventually I told my big sis, which was a big fat duh to her. She wasn't interested or disinterested. She had grown up with me, and she simply assumed that I had known all along that I was *different*. She had known all along, and yet we never talked about it. Heck, she probably understood *me* more than I did! And on that note, about my big sis, I did something that month that would indeed alienate the *one* person who always stood by my side. I banished her from my life over an argument that should have never happened. So now I had done it! And to myself no less! I had discarded the very person I needed so desperately throughout my life and whom I was about to need more than I had ever needed anyone. I gotta tell ya, the self-destructive things we do to ourselves baffle me to no avail! Nonetheless, my big sis and I were not speaking and I was about to learn the meaning of the word lonely, in a way I had never known before!

So on with my life I went, alone. Studying and learning all I could about what was happening to me. I became obsessed with lower lighting, candles, and incense. And that year I stopped playing the radio in my car. I used that time to speak with God and my Angels. And I still, to this day, do not turn the radio on in my car. Sometimes I will pop in a Doreen Virtue CD. That is actually how and when I learned to conduct very accurate past-life regression sessions. I loved my alone time, and I followed that Doreen Virtue person as much as I could. Over the Internet I could research her and learn. And learn I did! I trusted her. She didn't laugh at me. She gave me hope, so I clung to that person for all my knowledge. And I still do to this very day!

Mike and Lindy had their first baby in June of 2001—our granddaughter, Taylor. Life was moving along and I was in another part of the world. I was in a place where miracles happened, and I expected them, prayed for them, and manifested them! I was occupying space in this world that I never even knew existed!

The day before the 9/11 attack, a baby boy was born into this world. Not just any baby boy—but *my* baby boy! Although I had no idea he would become mine nor had I met him yet. He also had a seven-year-old brother who was soon to become mine as well. However, at the time, I had no clue this was going to happen either. I had absolutely no idea of the turn of events that were about to take place in my life. If I had—I may have run just as fast as I could to places unknown to humankind! But really, if we all take the time to think about it, none of us actually knows what the future holds, now do we? No, we truly don't. We can plan events and our futures as best we can, and we can try to direct our lives happily and accordingly—because I believe we are all in the pursuit of happiness—but none of us *really* knows exactly what our future holds. What an unsettling reality that is, huh? I mean when you really think about it. Well, I agree, but unsettling or not, it is life!

On the day that baby boy arrived here on this earth, I felt a nagging urge to go see him. I hadn't yet been given the opportunity to foster these two boys but I had a gut feeling (a knowing) that I might for reasons I cannot disclose in this story due to confidentiality. Oh—and of course, I did not tell Bob of my knowing. I truly had no desire to have any part of my husband succumbing to a heart attack. The youngest child of our four was sixteen and she was our last one at home, so why ever in the world would I have wanted or needed two more children? Ahhh, the many secrets our futures hold!

Anyway, it bothered me that entire day. I just had to go see this baby! So, by the time I got off work that evening, I had decided while riding my horse that I should go the next day and at least take a peek at this little fella. Well, I did indeed share this with Bob, and of course, he was less than pleased. He didn't agree. And—I didn't care. You know—they say that curiosity killed the cat. And all I have to say about that is: well—I'm not a cat! So there! No harm done!

The next morning, all hell broke loose. We, like everyone else in the entire world, were glued to the television set. We couldn't believe our eyes and what we were hearing! Terrorists? Suicide flights? The president was addressing the nation, our children were calling us, the phone lines were jammed, and they kept playing that horrible video of the plane hitting the first tower and then the second plane hitting the second tower. We clung to our family and we cried. And then we watched as the twin towers fell. And we, like the rest of our nation, were devastated!

Both Bob and I had to go to work that day. I owned a temporary staffing service at that time, and I knew that there were companies as well as employees who depended on me. Bob felt the same about his job. I didn't want to go, and I didn't want *him* to go. I wanted all my children to come home! I wanted us all to be together. Who didn't?

The next day, September 12, 2001, just before Bob walked out the door to go to work, he kissed me good-bye, and then, as though it were a last-minute thought, he had a Columbo moment as he paused, turned, and asked if I was going to go visit those boys. I told him especially in light of what was going on that I should. Tragedy can make even the most sane of folks do the most peculiar things. OK—peculiar is putting it mildly. Crazy would be more accurate. I mean honestly, I wasn't going to look at a couple of puppies at the pound! I told him I would indeed be going just to make an appearance. Hesitating at the door, he then turned back one last time and said, "Marti, don't you bring those kids home."

WHAT? I thought it was an absurd statement, and I told him so. "Why ever in the world would I do that?" I asked him.

"I don't know," he replied. He then, once again, asked me not to go. "You are too emotional," he pleaded.

Well, who in the heck did he think he was? I had my own mind and I wasn't stupid! And I surely didn't need a father! I was angry that he had so little faith in my judgment! I was insulted! However, he was correct in that I was very emotional. Everybody was!

That afternoon, I hesitantly drove to go see those boys. My thought was that I would go make an appearance and then leave. You know, give it the Good Old Mart once-over. Well, low and behold, someone else had a different plan for me, and this day would indeed change my life forever!

About an hour after I arrived to see the boys, I found myself standing in a boardroom of sorts with a social worker. I was given the opportunity to foster both children until they could be placed in a permanent home. It would really just take a few weeks. What would a few weeks out of my life hurt if it would help two children? Oh crud! I lived in a bubble!

I told the social worker that I would take the seven-year-old, because seven-year-olds are easy (and the shock would be less strenuous to Bob's immune system), but that I didn't want the baby. I had no way to care for a newborn.

She left me alone in that room, offering me the use of the telephone to call my husband while they ran an FBI check on me. I told her no. I didn't want to call my husband. He was about to become a "*was*-band," as I was about to become divorced!

Once alone in that room, I was scared to death. What was I doing! I was doing exactly what Bob had told me NOT to do! But surely he would understand. Wouldn't he? And it was only for a couple of weeks or however long it took for them to find him a foster home. And that is when they began to talk to me. My Angels. And I was once again in that place where time stood completely still.

These brothers will never know each other if they are separated. You have just one chance to make the right choice. The true choice. The unselfish choice.

The door opened and it startled me. It was the social worker and she was happy to report that I was cleared to take the older boy home. Before I even had time to think, before I even knew what was coming out of my own mouth, I blurted out that I would take the baby too!

The disbelief on her face surely reflected my own! "Are you sure?" she asked. No, quite frankly I wasn't sure of anything besides the fact that I would soon be divorced. Yes, I answered. I could not in good faith make a decision for that young boy and that baby that could affect the rest of their lives. It just wasn't my place to do so. They had to stay together!

I may not ever know exactly why I made that decision that day. But I have a pretty good idea. Hindsight and a whole lot of time and spiritualism have helped me piece things together. And now I'd like to share it with all of you.

When I was twenty-seven years old, I was told I had cervical cancer, that it was spreading to my uterus, and that they needed to operate right away. I would not be having any more children. The first thing out of my mouth was, "But I wanted to have another boy!" "You have four children," the doctor said. Be thankful. And I *was* thankful. But I wanted more. Just one more baby boy!

Throughout the years people have told me what a wonderful act of unselfishness I displayed that day. How lucky those boys were to have me. And I suppose to the untrained heart and eye it would seem so. But I know differently, because *I* was the one who had been graced with a gift that day. I asked for one more boy and I got *two more!* And those boys have changed my life.

I didn't go into a whole lot of detail regarding this miracle of events because I will be writing that book later on. I have promised both of my youngest sons, who are now twelve and nineteen, that I would write our story someday soon, so consider this as a prelude to a beautiful love story yet to be written.

My husband didn't divorce me, and to be quite truthful, there wasn't a darn thing I could have done if he had. I had made my choice—*their* choice actually. And all I can say to that is—now I know why. That will have to be good enough for now.

That was definitely a year of loneliness for me. My older children were not happy with the choices I had made in regard to my new children and—as we all know—neither was my husband. Everyone seemed to alienate me that year and yet, the more alone I became, the more peaceful I became. Isn't it funny how those around us seem to think they know what is best for us? Perhaps. Well, not funny really. That's simply a figure of speech. However, in my case, I know the resistance and disapproval from my older children and my husband came from a place of love, caring, and worry. I had, after all, gone off the deep end that year. I talked to and heard folks who couldn't be seen by others, I had alienated my big sis out of my life completely and at the age of forty-three, I took on two more children to raise. I did secret things with funny little cards behind closed doors and I studied things about the supernatural that were—well—just not natural at all! Well, to those from the outside looking in anyway.

The decision I made the day I brought the boys home was a knowing. It was a gut feeling that I knew beyond a shadow of anyone's doubt had to be carried out. I didn't know why. I simply knew it had to be! Yes, in my mind I knew it was absurd! Of course I did! But in my heart of hearts and in my knowing of all knowings, it was clear and it felt right. Even though my mind was telling me no! If there is anything to be learned from this story, please take heed of your knowing. Pay attention to it! There is a reason for that feeling of: *I don't know why I just have to*! I promise!

Oh—and just for the record, I patched things up with my big sis and took complete responsibility for my unbelievable actions. I had to! I needed her! And our separation taught me that little ditty, and I will never forget it! I honestly couldn't live without her! Thank God or whomever you choose to pray to that she loves me unconditionally or this story may have had a not-so-happy ending as you will soon come to find out.

Yup, a whole lot of things happened to me personally back in 2001. And it was indeed a very lonely time for me! And thirteen years later, as I look back now, it all makes perfect sense. It usually does when we look back if you really think about it. Gotta love that hindsight! Oh, and also for the record: loneliness *can* indeed be a four-letter word. **LONE!**

Dictionary Meaning: ***Lone***
Adjective: ***Standing by itself or apart; isolated: a lone house in the valley.***

Chapter Twelve

Manifestation

Or Is It—Imagination?

The next five years of my life were soul shattering, to say the least! It was as though I couldn't hear myself think! I felt as though I had to get busy, and I had to hurry! But hurry to do what? That was the question, as well as, why did I have to hurry at all? I felt like the earth was moving under my feet without me. And it was! It actually always is.

The house we had purchased in the country had a lot of land but the house itself was very small. We thought we could add on to it but later found out we couldn't, and it surely was not big enough to house Bob and me, our daughter, and two more children. However, we made the best of it, and it was a very cute little house, but the key word here is little!

Before I brought the boys home, when I took my horseback rides each morning and afternoon, I rode up and over the hill behind our house, which led me to another country neighborhood. Once I zigzagged through the sagebrush all the way up and then all the way down that mountain, it turned into a flat surface street. Each day, twice a day, I rode by this particular house that I truly loved. It was nothing special really. Well, perhaps not to someone other than me. To other passersby, it may have been just a house. But to me, it was a dream house—*my* dream house that I knew Bob and I could make into a Norman Rockwell-looking farmhouse if we could get our hands on something like that. I truly became obsessed with that house! Every time I rode down the mountain and that house came into my view, I began to say out loud, "That's a Bob and Marti house. That's going to be my house someday! That is my house!"

Well, low and behold, one afternoon while riding past *my* dream house, the gal who lived in the house with her husband was out planting flowers in a wagon that sat in the front yard. I had never met her in person before. She and her husband would wave to me every morning and every afternoon from their living room window when I rode by on my horse, but we had never spoken to one another until this particular day.

"I just love your house," I said to her as I rode up and stopped my horse on the street in front of her.

She stood up from planting her flowers and said, "Really? Because we are putting it on the market in the spring. It has become way too much house for us."

I couldn't believe my ears! I was so excited I gave her my business card, which I always carried in my saddlebags. (You never know who you might meet on the back of a horse, you know!) I told her to call me before she put it on the market. Then I rode home, put my horse away, fed him, and then went racing through the front door, telling Bob that my dream home was going up for sale!

He looked at me and after a longer pause than I cared for, he said, "Marti, we can't afford to live on that side of the hill."

I was devastated! Bob has always been the sensible one in our relationship and I have always been the dreamer. But his sensibility was beginning to wear on my last nerve, and that day, I really needed him to believe! To dream!

I looked up at him, and with my scolding finger near his face bouncing with each and every word, I said, "You aren't allowed to squash my dreams like that! I have been riding by that house for a year now, and I love that house! How do you know we can't afford it?" I quipped at him. "We don't even know what they would be asking for it."

I could see he didn't want to hurt my feelings—although he just may have wanted to slap some sense into me—but he didn't. No, he surely did not. He simply got very quiet and in a barely audible tone said, "Those homes are very expensive, and we have only lived here a year. We don't have enough equity built up in this house to sell it, babe."

Well, he had gone and done it once more! He had angered the notorious *babe—again*! Of course, he had been right about the kids, but who was keeping track? I mean besides me! So what! It didn't mean he was always right! Sheesh! So, I told him that it was *my* house, and I was going to own it! And that was that! He in turn, simply gave me that look he always gives me when he doesn't want to hurt my feelings (or slap the living hoopla right out of me), but I ignored him. And I began to daydream about what we could make that house look like. We could put a country front porch on it and put my horses out back. I had never even seen hide nor hair of the inside of that place, but I just knew I would love it! We had already remodeled two other homes throughout our sixteen-year marriage and I just *knew* what we could do with my new dream house. So, I continued to ride by it every day, and I said the very same thing out loud. "*That is my house!*"

One afternoon, shortly after I had met that woman who was living in *my* dream home, I received a call out of the blue from our Realtor asking if we wanted to sell our house. I was stunned. Sell it to who, I asked? He, also being a friend of ours, knew we couldn't add on to the house as we had planned, and he had received a call from a couple moving out from the Midwest, and they needed horse property very badly. He didn't even know about the boys. So, I explained to him our new situation and that, yes, I would love to sell the house and get a bigger one but we had only lived there a year. He said, "Well, what would you be asking for it?" I gave him a ridiculous price of thirty thousand dollars over what we had bought it for not even a year before that. He said he would talk to the potential buyers and get back to me. And he did, the very next day, and they accepted my offer! Holy smokes! I had just made thirty thousand dollars on a house we hadn't even lived in for a year! They needed us to be out in eight days, and I said OK. Oh, and then, I told Bob.

Well, low and behold I went riding over the hill a couple of days later and I couldn't believe my eyes, as there was a for sale sign in the front yard of my dream home! I panicked, called my Realtor from atop my horse (a lot sure can happen atop my horse!) on my cell phone, gave him the address, and asked him to look it up. At first he couldn't find the listing because I gave him the wrong street. Snap! Then I gave him the house street number that was proudly displayed on the address post, and he informed me it was another street I was on, but yes, he had pulled it up. I asked him to make an appointment for us to go see the house. I never even asked the price of the house! Oh—and as always—then I told Bob.

I think Bob simply agreed to go see the place to put my dream to rest once and for all. I think he felt I needed a reality check, so he appeased me. Perhaps. But I also think my Angels had another plan!

Well, we went to look at the house the very next day, and we both loved it! Yes, it would take a lot of work to make it what we wanted, but it was such a great house, and then they gave us the asking price. It was unbelievable! So, we offered them five thousand more than what they were asking to seal the deal. With our thirty thousand to put down from the house we just sold, we could actually make this work, and our payment wasn't that far off what we had been paying on the other house!

We needed to make some arrangements. We had to rent another house for eight weeks. The owners of my dream house needed that long to move out, and we had to be out of our existing house within six more days. No problem, I rented a farmhouse out in the valley, and we waited it out.

On December 8, 2001, we moved into my manifested dream home! My miracle! My proof to Bob and the entire world that my Angels were indeed very real and that you can manifest anything you want if only you *BELIEVE*!

I have always felt that my Angels handed me that house on a silver platter because I took those boys home and loved them like my own. Oh, and just for the record, so did Bob! Those two young boys and Bob became inseparable. I had indeed been *very* worried about space on the day I (they) made the choice to bring two more children home. And I choose to believe it is so. No matter what the reason, the end result was the same. That house became legally ours and eventually, so did the boys.

After we moved into the bigger house, the demolition began and we have been adding to and remodeling this house ever since. And we have loved every moment we have spent here. The boys have now grown up here as well as our grandchildren. Yes, a miracle indeed! Some *may* and *have* called it a coincidence. And that would be fine and well except for one slight, minuscule problem—I don't believe in coincidences. Never have and never will!

Chapter Thirteen

My Calling

If it's a Calling—Then Why Are You Yelling?

THE NEXT PHASE I experienced in my life was an incredible urge to conduct funerals. Yes, for heaven's sakes, you read it right—funerals! I didn't want to be the one who got up and spoke at funerals any longer. I wanted to *officiate* at them. I had been asked periodically throughout my life to get up and speak at funerals. I always had such beautiful things to say about the dearly departed. In all actuality, I knew exactly what to say because they were never really *my* words; however, I wouldn't put that little ditty together for quite some time. So, I began to study, and I became an ordained chaplain. Once I did that, I realized I could take seminary classes. And so I did! I got my degree in spiritualism first, then metaphysics, then metaphysical healing, and then my doctorate in divinity, my master's in spiritual leadership, and then eventually, my life coaching license. I am still furthering my education to this day. I do so love to learn!

Each time I received a degree in the mail, I would open it up, look at it, and then place it in my desk drawer. I had no clue why I was taking all these classes, other than the simple fact that I truly *needed* and *wanted* to learn! And learn I did! Years later, *The Secret* would come out in print as well as on DVD, and I would discover that I had indeed manifested much of what had already happened to me. If you believe it, then you can achieve it! I wasn't really sure I understood all the metaphysical aspects of things, as I tend to lean more toward the spiritual side of life, but I knew without a doubt that there just had to be something to all of this. The big question was what the something was and what the heck did the term *all of this* entail?

And just for the record: metaphysics is simply unseen energy. And—my opinion is, so is spiritualism!

In December of 2005, my mom became very sick. I had sold my temporary staffing service about a year prior and began working from home as a private recruiter, conducting job placements. I had just applied for my ordination, and my mom had just broken her back. I wasn't very close to my mother, so I went to see her only a couple of times in the hospital. I regret that now. I called the hospital to check on her progress every once in a while. I also called and spoke to her quite often over the phone. But to be honest, I could never take anything my mother said seriously; therefore, I simply assumed it was all exaggerated. Sounds horrible, I know, but growing up in my family, well, everything was always exaggerated. My big sis, Jodie, and I seemed to be the only ones left in our family of so many. Sometimes, I truly think it is easier to lose a loved one to death than it is to lose them to life. Sad—yes—so very sad indeed.

At the same time my mom was trying to go through rehab for her back, I broke my ankle. Actually, I shattered it so badly that I had to have surgery, or I would have never walked on it again. It was December 14, 2005. On December 20, I had a three-hour surgery to put my ankle back to together. Two steel plates and seventeen screws later, I was in rehab myself! It was an eight-month recovery, and all I have to say about that is God sure works in mysterious ways!

During my recovery, as well as what was supposed to be my mother's recovery, she decided that she didn't want to go through rehab. Nope—she wanted to die. She decided that she was going to stop taking all her medications for her heart, pacemaker, diabetes, and everything else she was taking that was keeping her alive. At the age of seventy-nine, she simply didn't want to be here anymore. Fair enough, I suppose, and her reasons were locked away in my heart as the secrets of all untold secrets. It was a very sad and frustrating time in my life. And had I not been laid up myself, I know I would have forced her to go through rehab. I would have pulled her out of that bed and made her want to live! Sure I would have! And just as soon as I had accomplished that task, I would then probably have created another entire universe! What a dreamer! However, not only could I not drive at the time, I could not place any weight on my ankle for six months, so I was on crutches, but for some strange reason, we also had the worst snow we had seen in years that winter. Most days the roads were so bad that, broken ankle or not, I would not have made the trek into town anyway. However, I must say that I tried.

The first day I decided to go visit my mother, Jane, a friend of mine who keeps her horse at my house, came over to take me to the hospital to see my mom. As I was getting ready, she yelled to me from the kitchen that one of the burner lights was on but the burner didn't seem to be. I hobbled up the stairs on my bottom from my family room to the kitchen and then stood with my crutches and took a look at it. Yep, the burner light was surely on but the burner wasn't. So, I set my crutches up against the counter and leaned on the island to get a better look at the cooktop. I then reached to simply turn the burner knob and the entire thing exploded! It threw me backward and I fell against the far counter. Trying desperately not to come down on my bad ankle, I hopped on my good leg, trying to catch my balance, but to no avail. I came down on my boot not just once—but twice! It was awful pain, and afterward I sat down on the stairway and cried. It had frightened me and the stove was still flickering flames.

I took my boot off and checked to make sure my screws hadn't pierced through my skin. I hate to take pain pills so I put my leg up on pillows, trying to alleviate the pain that day, and that is where I stayed. I could always go and see my mom another day. So I made arrangements with Jane to try it again the next day. It would be her day off again, and so we simply moved our visit to the following day. Jane really liked my mom and wanted to go see her as well. Plans were made again.

Later on that night I realized that in all the commotion, I had thrown my back out. That too was very painful. So I slept sitting up in the leather chair in my family room that night with my leg propped up and a heating pad on my back, not wanting to move! The muscle spasms were horrible. I took a pain pill against my better judgment and fell asleep only to wake up to my back on fire. One of the gel packs had fallen out of the heating pad and was burning my back! After quite a struggle to get up, I grabbed my crutches and went into the bathroom. I lifted the back of my shirt and took a look in the mirror, horrified at what I saw! Blisters had formed along my side and the small of my back where the gel packs had been. So it was back to the doctor the next day. He swore we needed to put me in a bubble! I had third-degree burns on my back, and I had indeed thrown my back out. I was miserable! And the thought of visiting my mother became the furthest thing from my mind.

A couple of days later, my mom's doctor called me and proceeded to yell at me, explaining to me that my mother was totally capable of healing and that I must try to talk some sense into her. Uh huh—my mother? When my mother set her mind to something, she darn well did it, and that was that! However, I had a long, heartfelt talk with my mom over the phone from the convalescent hospital where they had her in custody, and she truly and honestly *did* want to die. She begged me to call hospice and have her evaluated, which I did. And the verdict was—that my mom was done! So the decision was made to move her home to die.

I truly thought this was just another ploy for my mom to break out of the hospital. I really did not believe that my mom was quitting. My mother may have been a lot of things during her time here on this earth, but being a quitter was certainly not one of those things! However, I would come to learn—and very quickly, I might add—that she was indeed quitting.

Once they moved her home, she went back and forth a lot from one day to the next. One day, she was going to get better and the next day, she just wanted to die. This was the Mary I had come to know and love. Well, to the best of my ability anyway.

Jodie and our mother hadn't really spoken for years. If there happened to be a conversation, it was Jodie yelling at her, and my mom, well, saying absolutely nothing. Jodie had been taking care of me and nursing me back to health while my mother had made all these death decisions on her own behalf. Jodie would sit in silence as I spoke to our mother over the phone. She, like me, thought it was just another ploy for attention by our mom. And I know that sounds just truly awful but our mother had set the stage for this pattern of behavior a long time before that, in a land far away.

Her caretaker called one afternoon to say that our mother was dying. Her caretaker had EMT training so when our mom coded, she performed CPR. Our mom had a DO NOT RESUSCITATE (DNR) order, but I suppose that just might go right out the window with yesterday's trash when someone has stopped breathing. And it did. And she revived her. And our mother was madder than a hornet! That is the day Jodie decided to step in.

I suppose now is as good a time as any to let you all in on a little secret. OK, a pretty big epiphany, but who's keeping track? I mean, besides us.

I shattered my ankle socket stepping out of my truck at my mother's house the day we called the paramedics to have her moved to a convalescent hospital so that she could go through rehab. That was *my* decision (not the breaking of my ankle, but putting my mom in rehab). I reckon someone was trying to tell me something. Like perhaps, stay out of it! You are intruding! Upsetting the balance of things! You are getting in the way of Divine Order! Or something along those lines, I'm quite certain. Not to mention the fact that I stepped down out of my truck onto a speed bump! I did not realize that I had parked directly over that darn thing until I heard my leg crack like a tree branch, and I hit the ground like a sack of potatoes! It wouldn't be until later on that I would put all this together. Speed bumps are placed in certain areas to slow us down and this one just happened to be right out in front of my mother's mobile home! Coincidence? Well, we all know better than to ask *me* that question, now don't we? I suppose they had to set me down long and hard to keep me from getting in the way.

As I began to explain earlier, Jodie decided to step in after our mother's caretaker decided to bring our mother back to life against her own wishes. If nothing else, Jodie was determined to either make our mother live or allow her to die but one or the other needed to happen, and Jodie felt *that* to be our mother's decision! It was time for the eldest daughter of Ed and Mary Littlefield to get involved. So, one snowy morning, Jodie showed up at my house like clockwork to feed the horses and tend to whatever I might need on that particular day, and she decided that we were going over there.

"Over where?" I asked.

"Over to Mom's," she not so gently told me.

"Why?" I asked.

"Because someone needs to tend to her," was all she said. Now, this was extremely out of the norm for Jodie. Why ever in the world would Jodie care about our mother? Nonetheless, I got myself ready, and with much hesitation I was indeed going over to our mother's house with Jodie. To do what—I had no clue.

So, she practically carried me out to her car because of the snow and ice and got me placed in the front seat and then went to walk around to get into the driver's seat and—she fell! She slipped on the ice in the driveway and went down on her back! That is when it all came together. The fall at my mom's house, throwing my back out, the burns, all of it! In one brief moment I received it all! Great! First thing I had to do was get out of the car somehow and find my big sister, who had been there one minute and gone the next!

I opened my car door screaming for her!

"Jodie, where are you?" I frantically cried out.

The snowdrifts alongside the driveway had to be three feet high and it was freezing outside!

"I'm right here." She groaned from directly under my open car door.

"Are you OK?" I asked through gut-wrenching sobs.

"Stop crying, Mart, I'm fine." She groaned again as she tried to get up.

"We shouldn't go, Jodie," was all I could get out of my mouth.

They didn't want us to intervene!

"Don't you see? That is why I hurt myself! Mom was meant to leave this place like this. The way she has chosen. They do not want us interfering!"

She grabbed on to the inside of my door handle, slip-sliding as she tried to pull herself up.

I reached down and grabbed her arm. She was grunting and groaning, and then my tears turned to laughter as she said, "Was that incoming message so all-fire important that it couldn't wait until I was off my back in the driveway? Or do you think your little friends could have been kind enough to tell you this epiphany before we walked outside?"

She was now standing next to my open car door hunched over, hanging on for dear life, trying to catch her breath.

"Did they tell you they were going to break my back too?" She laughed.

"I'm not kidding," I said through laughter as well as tears. "*I'm not!*" I insisted. "We have been holding up progress," I said as though I had just invented the microwave oven.

"Well, do you think they could have told you before they tried to kill me?" she asked. "Can I get in the car before we discuss this grand information of yours?" she scoffed. "I'm freezing and I think I'm hurt!"

She skated around the hood of the car, hugging it as though she had somehow fallen in love with the grill, scooted down to her side of the car, opened her door, and got in. Still breathing heavily and obviously hurting, she simply held on to the steering wheel in silence as she gazed out through the windshield. And we sat in silence for about ten minutes. And ten minutes can be a really long time in silence. Well, for me anyway.

Jodie finally spoke after gathering her thoughts.

"Are you sure, Mart?" she asked exhaling as though she was thoroughly and completely tired of me.

"I am, Jodie. I have never been so sure about anything in my life."

Silence again.

"Well then, we will let her die but someone has to make sure she is comfortable and properly medicated. Someone has to take charge over there, Mart."

Jodie had always hated our mother. I realize that hate is such a strong and awful word, but she had justifiable cause to hate in this situation. *Another book, I promise!* This was a new behavior for her in regard to our mother. I always thought in the most secret part of my mind that Jodie would have wished a slow and painful death for our mother, and that too is an awful statement to make but also so very understandable.

I learned a lot about my big sister that day. I always received unconditional love from Jodie. She was the oldest and she was very motherly toward me. I knew her soft side. But our mother had never seen or felt the kindness of that side of Jodie. Ah, but she was about to meet her true eldest daughter for the first time. The real Jodie turned the key in the ignition and we headed over to our mother's home.

I suppose once Jodie had made it clear that she had no intention of stopping death, and that she would keep the ever-so-popular me in check, that the Angels probably decided to allow the upcoming chain of events to actually happen. Of course, I think they already knew. They know everything. It was me who had to understand that we were not going to make her live, but we were going to make her as comfortable as possible so that she could die. Yes, it was indeed, once again, undeniably, *my* lesson!

Chapter Fourteen

Another Ending

That's All, Folks!

I HAVE TO ADMIT that during the short ride over to our mother's house, my mind was reeling with anticipation; the anxiety was overwhelming. I was so afraid that our mother would be—well, I was afraid that she might yell at Jodie to get out! My mother's final chance to get the last word in.

When we pulled up in front of our mother's tiny little house, we sat in the car once again in silence. Our mother's caretaker had moved her from her trailer into a cute little house while our mom had been in the convalescent hospital. Not a speed bump in sight!

We both just sat in the car staring at that house as though it were breathing. And I suppose in a strange sort of way, it was. Both of us just sat there in silence, staring at this house that truly harbored the ending of all endings! I'm sure both of us were taking a nice leisurely stroll down memory lane, as neither one of us seemed to want to race to our dying mother's bedside. Who does that?

It was early in the morning, and I usually love early mornings, but I surely didn't like that particular early morning. Let's face it, folks, it hadn't exactly started out all that great.

After about five minutes, I broke the silence by asking if we were going to get out of the car. Reasonable question, don't you think?

Jodie took in a deep breath, and then she exhaled her answer, "I guess," as she reached for the door handle.

We had to get me out of the car and then get me over the snow drifts along the sidewalk. That was a feat by itself. Once we accomplished that task, we were walking up the walkway to the house. Well, I was hobbling on crutches and Jodie was walking.

There were two entrances. One to the front door and the other to our mother's room; however, we had no idea that we could use that entrance, so we had to try the front door first. No one answered, so we stepped around the other side of the house to the second entrance. Through the large picture window, we could see the caretaker tending to our mother. She was happy to see us and opened the door. I was scared to death! I was just waiting for the fireworks and the yelling that always ensued when my mom and Jodie were in the same room together.

Our mom was sleeping in a hospital bed and when we entered the room there wasn't a whole lot of space. The caretaker announced to our mom that she had visitors, and I thought I might clench my jaw so tightly that I just might have broken my own teeth.

Our mom stirred and opened her eyes. Jodie was the first to her bedside, and our mom simply began to cry, saying Jodie's name over and over again. "My Jodie," she was crying as Jodie went to our mother and embraced her, crying as well. So much for my psychic insight!

As Jodie's face was embedded in our mother's neck I couldn't hear exactly what was being said between the two of them, but Jodie was muffling that it was OK, she was there now. I was crying because I suppose that is what I do best in such situations. A healing was taking place before my very eyes that I never in my wildest imagination could have ever fathomed I would see. Not in this lifetime anyway! And once that soggy muffled greeting was over, Jodie stood up and looked around and asked the caretaker to explain to her what was going on.

She was briefed, and then she did what Jodie does best. She took charge. And that began a two-week vigil of bedside posts: me on the morning shift, Jodie in the afternoons, and the caretaker on nights.

Most of the time, Jodie was there all day. But if she had to leave, I was there to sit by our mother's bedside to tend to her.

Our mother went out of this world in the worst pain I have ever witnessed and I hope to *never* witness it *ever* again in my life! Because she had been sedentary for so long and she had stopped taking her insulin, myopathy had set in and she hurt everywhere. And she had bedsores that Jodie tended to every day. I sat by her bedside each day watching her catheter tube turn from yellow to orange and then to red. I knew it wouldn't be long after that.

One morning, shortly after we arrived, our mother told Jodie that her friend was there.

"Whose friend?" Jodie asked, perplexed.

"Your friend," our mother replied to her.

"She is pretty, you know, he murdered her! Jackie is her name," our mom continued as though Jackie had just called and left a message!

Jodie couldn't move! Her friend Jackie had indeed been murdered many years before that but our mother didn't know her here in this place. I was mesmerized! This was right up my alley! It fascinated me! That same day, our mom woke up from a sound sleep and propped herself up and began waving and pointing at something across the room. I was once again enthralled as I watched our mom point and slightly wave.

Very quietly I asked her, "Who are you waving at, Mom?"

And just as though that was the dumbest question she had ever heard, she answered, "Well, it's Gammy and Pop!"

Gammy and Pop? Those were my father's parents! Gammy and Papa!

Why wouldn't she see her own parents, I wondered?

"Where are they, Mom?" I whispered.

"Well, they are right there in the chair," she answered as though I were stupid! "Can't you see them?" she asked.

"Gammy is sitting in the chair and Pop is standing next to her."

Well, quite frankly, no, I couldn't see them. However, somewhere in that deep part of my knowing, I felt a presence. There was no doubt that someone was sitting or standing or taking up space in that very section of the room.

Our mom had always loved our father's parents. They were good to her. And she had loved his mother deeply. And they had loved her! Papa and our mother had parted ways after she and our father divorced. He was angry with her. She had hurt our father. But Gammy was always very respectful toward our mother. She was always the forgiving one of any soul who had ever done wrong here in this place. Gammy never judged or hated anyone. Just the same, why them? Why not my mom's own parents? This seemed most peculiar indeed. It wouldn't be until just a few years later that I would learn that we don't get to pick who comes to visit. They are, after all, on the other side, and they can darn well do as they please! Like Jackie showing up. Why? Why her? Oh my goodness, did I have a lot to learn, and learn I would. All in due time.

One afternoon, Jodie was out running errands, and I was sitting by our mother's bedside with my boot propped up on a pillow, reading a book, when all a sudden, our mom broke the silence in the room by saying my name. She hadn't spoken clearly in almost a week, and it scared me.

"I'm here," I said as I reached over and touched her arm.

And just as though we had been having a conversation all along, she told me, "You need to pursue your gift."

My gift? My gift? What gift?

"What do you mean?" I asked her. She had never uttered those words to me in my entire life! She had never acknowledged that *what was wrong with me*, was a gift! I was just a great storyteller! I was a liar who told stories for attention. And just as clearly as if she had never shut down, she told me she was sorry that she had stifled me. She went on to explain that she had been afraid of it when I was a small girl, but that it was now time for me to help others. *They want you to.*

I was in shock! And had she just said, *THEY* as in *THEY, my Angels,* or *THEY,* meaning those on the other side? And *they* wanted me to do exactly what again? Pursue my gift, huh? My gift that had never really existed?

"Who?" I asked her. "Who wants me to, Mom?"

"Your friends," she answered. "It is your time now."

I had not told my mom that I had just applied for my ordination. I never discussed anything with her at all regarding my personal or spiritual beliefs.

I wanted to run screaming through the streets! Did you hear her? She said that *THEY* want me to pursue my gift! And I just may have, had I not had my broken ankle in a recuperating boot!

I told her I was. That I had been studying, and that I knew I was meant to do something more.

She then asked me if I believed in hell.

"No," I told her, "I don't, Mom."

"Good," she said.

"Why?" I asked her.

"Because I am afraid, Marti. I am afraid to die."

OK, stop the world, because I'm getting off! This coming from the woman who wished all her life that she would wake up dead. That she hated life and us and everything else in between. She, our mother, was afraid to die? Huh boy! I was so confused I think I needed to throw up! But I didn't. No, I simply did what I do best. I consoled her.

"Don't be afraid, Mom," I nurtured. "It is beautiful on the other side. Just release and let go and they will take it from there. There is no reason to be afraid."

"Will *he* be there?"

"Who?" I asked, most perplexed.

"That son of a bitch who hurt you and Jodie," she answered.

OK, hold the phone! She was referring to our stepfather, the monster. I was shocked. Not only had she just called him a son of a bitch, which was truly not uncommon, but she had clearly admitted for the first time in her life that he had hurt us!

"I will never forgive him for what he did to you and Jodie, and I will never forgive myself for allowing it."

OK now she was talking about the molestation, which was always *Marti's way of getting attention*, according to our mother! And she was what? Atoning for her sins? Admitting that it *had* been true, that she knew about it, and that she was—*sorry? And never mind that! Jodie had never told anyone but me! So how did she know about Jodie?*

Once again, I comforted her and I told her that I supposed he would be there but not like she knew him here. "He will be different there, Mom. His lessons here in this place were finished, and now he is loving energy. You will not be afraid, and you will not have these same feelings on the other side, Mom," I assured her.

"I don't want to see him," she said with her eyes closed and clearly growing tired of talking now.

"Then you won't," I said.

"Are you sure, Marti?" She sounded so childlike. So scared. This was a strange happening for me. This woman who had always been so strong, so sure of herself, and well, so darned mean!

"Yes, Mom, I am sure," I answered her most sincerely. Because I was sure! I knew he was no longer who he had been in this place. I also knew that once she crossed over, she would know this too. But I just couldn't explain it to her here. She would have to see for herself.

Was this why she had been holding on to this world for so long? Was she frightened that she would see *him?*

"Dad will be there too, Mom," I told her. "And your parents and Gammy and Papa. All those whom you have loved and lost here in this place will be there, Mom," I assured her. And then she said it. The words I never thought I would hear come out of her mouth.

She said, "I should have never left your father."

Holy smokes! I couldn't believe my ears! I could feel the tears welling up in my eyes, and I could feel my throat closing because all I could think of at that moment was I wondered if my dad was listening. Did you hear that, Dad? I thought to him. All he ever lived for was to hear those words come out of her mouth and she finally said them! He had been dead for *thirteen years* by that time. *T-h-i-r-t-e-e-n years.* The very same number of years they had been married. Coincidence? OK—not again!

There *was* just one more time shortly after that day that our mom spoke again. She woke up out of a sound sleep and informed Jodie and

A Whisper in the Wings

I that she had to get to work! She was trying to sit up but the pain was unbearable. All she could do was cry! "The baby needs milk," she had said in a panic.

Jodie and I, one on each side of her bed, assured her that we had already gotten milk.

"How?" She snapped the question at us with her eyes still closed. And there was the Mary we had all come to know and love!

After a brief and panicked pause, I told her that Jodie had gotten a job and that she had bought milk for the baby. She laid back after that, mumbling that Jodie was a good girl.

Soon after that conversation, on the very same day, she opened her eyes just briefly, asking us if we knew about a pony she had been given by her father when she was a girl.

We both, once again looked at each other as though we had been thrown into the twilight zone. "No," Jodie finally said. "What was his name?"

She struggled with the pony's name before she finally gave up on trying to remember it, but she remembered that her dad never let her ride that pony. "He gave it to me, and then he never let me ride."

It made me feel sad. Sad and yet more understanding of the angry, uncaring woman she had been here in this place. Not always, but most of the time. I believe I cursed a dead man under my breath that day before she finally fell back to sleep.

Our mom didn't say a whole lot after that day. She cried a lot because of the pain. Jodie kept her pretty sedated and comfortable with the help of a young hospice nurse. I knew for sure we just had to be getting close. Her catheter bag had been blood red for three days.

The day before my mom crossed over, I informed her that Jodie would be taking the morning shift and that I would be there later in the afternoon the next day. I told her it was Bob's birthday and that we were going to breakfast. My mom loved Bob, and she repeated what I said and quite clearly. "Oh, it's Bobby's birthday tomorrow?" she asked. "Tell Bobby happy birthday for me," she said, just as plain as day. Just as though we had been having a nice conversation over coffee.

The next morning, as Bob and I were heading out the door, the phone rang and I knew. Bob answered the phone and it was Jodie. His face turned stone white. There was a deafening silence in my family room and a very long pause before he handed me the phone. "Your mom just passed," he said, still holding the phone. "It's Jodie."

I took the phone and the first thing out of my mouth was, "Are you sure?"

"Yes," Jodie said. "I'm sure, Mart. She died in my arms."

How profound, I thought.

"I'm on my way," I told her.

"I was in the middle of bathing her so I want to finish getting her gown on her and," she paused. "I closed her eyes, Mart. She opened her eyes just before she exhaled for the last time and she looked right at me with such a serene look on her face. As though she were looking right at me with a knowing."

"Did she look scared, Jodie?" I asked.

"No," Jodie said. "She looked like she had surrendered. She looked peaceful. She looked directly into my eyes."

And that was that! My mom died on Bob's birthday in Jodie's arms! Shows just how little we all know here in this place. Quite frankly, I had always made a joke that our mother would go out of this world on some major holiday like Christmas just to get attention, because that is who she was. I guess that was my come-uppins, as my dad would have said. The word karma, didn't exist in his vocabulary nor in his day.

I learned many new, amazing things that winter. One of those things being that no one dies on my watch! I have done last rites at the hospital since that day, and I have officiated at many funerals, but I have never seen anyone exhale a last breath. It isn't my path. It just isn't my particular calling. I have been known to actually tell my clients and friends that if they get sick and they aren't ready to go, just call me! No one dies on my watch!

Another most profound thought occurred to me the day our mother died as I sat in the driveway in a lawn chair, in the warmth of that beautiful February morning, waiting for the little white van to arrive and retrieve her body. Ready? OK, here we go! We all leave in the little white van! Unless you actually drop dead at the funeral home, we all leave in that *little white van!* Perhaps there is some sort of insightful truth in that human race thing? Maybe we *are* all in a race! A race to the final finish line. And perhaps, just perhaps, those of us who get there first are indeed the true winners. Something to ponder I suppose. Oh, and you surely don't need a fast car to get there! Nope, you don't even need a car nor do you really even need the little white van! In all truthfulness, the little white van simply shows up to accommodate the aftermath as a courtesy.

My mother crossed over on the tenth of February 2005. Four days later, I received my ordination certification in the mail. It was dated: February 10, 2005. Coincidence? Honestly? Must we?

Chapter Fifteen

Signs and Messages

Get a Billboard Already!

THE DAY AFTER the death of our mother, it poured rain. Jodie came over to my house and we sat together in my living room on the couch staring out the big picture window, and we cried. We cried for the mother we never had and we cried for the mother we had only come to know for the last three weeks of her life. We cried for the grace of second chances and we cried just because it felt good to do so!

We discussed signs that day. All the signs and happenings that had been thrown at us, screamed at us! We talked about the day I shattered my ankle and how everything just continued to put roadblocks or *speed bumps* in our way in our desperate attempt to save our mother's life.

I was still very confused and not willing to admit yet that I just may have something going on inside myself. Well, of course by that time, I had a pretty darn good idea, but I was still very nervous about admitting it.

After Jodie left that day, I continued to sit on the couch for hours and just watch the rain. I love the rain! Always have. It soothes me. I began to think back on all I have shared with you thus far. And I realized that they had been giving me signs all along the way. They do this for all of us. But the key is to pay attention. For heaven's sake. I felt like I needed to wear a big fat DUH sign on my forehead!

I thought back on all the years and all the times I had sidestepped their guidance. And once I began, I couldn't stop! My gosh, there were hundreds and hundreds of times they tried to tell me! Fear will make us do the darndest things. Or *not* do the darndest things. Whichever you prefer.

Why didn't I listen? How could I not have seen? And then I got a thought. Timing. It is always timing. Ah! And what I would learn about timing over the next seven years would blow my mind! Of course, I didn't know that then. Up until that point in my life, time was just something that went forward by the hands of the clock. And *timing* was important only if you were running a race.

In my car, the shower and my laundry room is where I get most of my messages. Well, and in my session's room. I suppose it is because in those places I am alone with only my thoughts. Unless I have a client in my room—but even then, I still feel like it is only *them*, the client and me. Sometimes as I am approaching home, I feel so peaceful with all my unseen friends that I tend to want to pass up my driveway and continue driving to who knows where. And for who knows how long. I love that feeling. I always have and I always will.

If we pay attention—not become obsessed, but truly pay attention—such as while we are driving, several signs and messages will come to us. A license plate or a billboard or even an obstacle in the road may have meaning. I pay special attention to speed bumps, but I suppose that would be a no-brainer at this point of the story. What we think is a wrong turn can sometimes lead us to the right place. Ever notice that? Where we thought we were supposed to be going, turns out not to be so. Funny how that happens sometimes.

Paying attention is the key. Signs versus Coincidence. Let me show you the difference.

Sign
Noun
1. **A token; indication.**
2. **Any <u>object</u>, action, event, pattern, etc., that conveys a meaning.**

3. A conventional or arbitrary mark, figure, or symbol used as an <u>abbreviation</u> for the <u>word</u> or words it represents.
4. A motion or gesture used to express or convey an idea, command, <u>decision</u>, etc.: *Her nod was a sign that it was time to leave.*
5. A notice, bearing a <u>name</u>, direction, warning, or advertisement, that is displayed or posted for public view: *a traffic sign; a store sign.*

Co·in·ci·dence
Noun
1. A striking occurrence of two or more events at one time apparently by mere chance: *Our meeting in Venice was pure coincidence.*
2. The condition or fact of <u>coinciding</u>.
3. An instance of this.

Synonyms
1. Accident, Luck, Fate.

Quite a difference, huh? However, this is simply my account or my *perception*. But we have been referring to that Mr. Webster guy all our lives to determine the meanings of words. And even me, Marti, cannot alter his dictionary. And I just typed it out in black and white. Although I think I could add a couple of words. Such as: Halle-flippin-luiah! My dad would be proud!

Signs and messages are everywhere. Again, I will remind you to pay attention. Try not to dismiss the obvious when it is staring you in the face! If it strikes you as a coincidence, that's a sign or a message. Plain and simple.

Pennies, butterflies, birds, feathers, a wrong number with a familiar name, a thought that isn't your own, delays due to missing keys, dreams, flickering lights, street-lamps that go out as you pass by them, and I could go on and on. However, I'm sure you get the picture. And pay attention to who comes to mind when these things happen. It may just be someone you once knew!

Communicating with the other side, whether with those who have crossed over or our Angels, is quite precise and a knowing in your tummy that can't be ignored! So don't! It is the only way they know how to get through to us. Well without scaring the living bejesus out of us anyway. So let them communicate! You have nothing to lose and EVERYTHING to gain! Allow those beliefs into your life and watch your life change! I can tell you from experience; it sure beats the heck out of the alternative!

Chapter Sixteen

Timing

If I Could Save Time in a Bottle—I'd Get Drunk!

Timing. What a huge subject for such a mundane word. Most of us don't really think about time or timing unless we have somewhere to be at a certain time, which most of us do. But you know, if we had no clocks, and if all we had to go by was the position of the sun or the moon or daylight and darkness, just think how much less stressful life would be. Time. Quite frankly, it has always been a thorn in my side. I have always tended to be just on time or *fashionably late*. I learned that great phrase from TV. *Fashionably late.* Has a nice ring to it now, doesn't it? Well, it gets me off the hook in most cases, so I like it.

Time has always bothered me. Being told that if I don't hurry I am going to be late has always rubbed my hide the wrong way! How can we be late when we are right where we are supposed to be? I suppose in the real world, that statement sounds rather, well, silly. I mean, take a wedding for instance. If we are late for a wedding we will miss the big moment! But if we truly think about it, that big moment is going to happen, come heaven or high water, when it was darn well supposed to happen, with or without us! Unless of course, we are the bride or the groom, in which case, that big moment will not happen at all—which only means—it wasn't meant to happen *at that particular time*. Complicated? It doesn't have to be.

We put so much emphasis on time that it rules our lives. My gosh, we are all on such a hurried time schedule in this place that it is a wonder that most of us don't have ulcers! And yes, I too play into this just like the rest of us. Always have to be somewhere *on time.*

My big sis Jodie, always tells me we have to be somewhere an hour before we actually do because she knows she has to trick me so I will be ready. Been that way ever since I can remember, and I suppose there is a good reason for that, thus the writing of this chapter.

There is no time on the other side. Here, let me type that again. *There is no time on the other side!* Why would there be? Like, where do they have to be except exactly where they are?

"Ever since the beginning of time," is a very popular saying. Well, ever since the beginning of *my time*, I have dillydallied my way through life. I have been late, I have been on time, and I have been fashionably late. *I just love that phrase!* I can't truly remember an instance when I have been early unless I made a mistake. I hate to be early. I hate waiting around for something to happen.

I can remember when I was a young girl, walking through the snow to school back in Ohio. *And no, it wasn't uphill both ways!* Anyway, I would zigzag my way through the snow, focusing more on the creative trail I was leaving rather than getting to school on time! Heck! School was going to start with or without me so what was the big deal? Well, to Jodie, it was a huge deal! And it still is! "Hurry up," she would yell at me all the way to school. And most times, if she had focused on getting to school instead of waiting on me, she would have saved herself a lot of stress! And by the way, *we were right on time* every day. I was always to my class just as the bell rang, *and not a second before!*

My mom used to say, you will be late to your own funeral! Now I ask you, what in the heck kind of a statement is that? So what! I won't be there anyway! *People* are not just late to their own funerals, but they are downright "No Call-No Shows"! I think that is a hoot! My last hurrah! And just for the record, I won't be attending *that* function at all! Well, not here anyway.

Timing is everything. That is another phrase we hear a lot, and *that* one just so happens to be one I agree with. Knowing what I now know and what I have learned over the past eight years, I am convinced that it is indeed what rules this planet. Not to be confused with *time* but *time-ing!* Huge difference indeed!

Timing is what makes the difference in a near death or actual death. Timing is what matters when it comes down to everything we do! Being at the right time in the right place or the wrong time in the wrong place or the wrong time in the right place—well you get the picture. There is another old saying that goes: If the dog hadn't stopped to, well do its business, it would have caught the rabbit. I don't believe that! The dog wasn't meant to catch the rabbit if he took the time to, well, do his business! And I cleaned that phrase up real well just for the sake of this book!

Now, everyone in times of sorrow and experiencing the loss of a loved one has heard the expression: It was just their time. Well, even though most of us say this just because we have no other explanation, and it makes us feel better, that statement is actually truer than truth itself!

We are all allotted a certain amount of time (moments) here on this earth and when our moments are up, we leave. We are finished, task completed, The End! And the real kicker is: we chose it! We chose it before we got here! Now I know what you are all thinking. Why? Why in the name of God would a baby choose to be born still, or better known as stillborn. Not breathing. Well, that's the million-dollar question, which is our own journey for whatever reason. Who is to say why some of us stay for 105 years and some of us only moments or no moments at all? I suppose there is a good reason for all of it but the frustrating truth is, is that we won't truly know until we, ourselves, cross back over. Then we get it and we understand it completely. I learn more from listening to my deceased friends than I ever could listening to an instructor here on this earth.

So, now that we have a pretty good indication of how timing is of the essence, I can move forward with my story, and I hope I have enlightened you in some way to get your minds working in a whole new direction. It will help you to understand how the rest of my journey took on a mind of its own.

When I talk to those who have crossed over, or someone's Angels, there is no time, just serenity. The dead, or as I prefer to call them, entities, don't know how long they have been gone from this place. They do, however, know seasons. I use seasons to explain to them how long they have been gone—and, yes—they always ask! To them, everything is right now and in the moment. If they knew time, they would be waiting for us, longing for us to come and be with them; quite frankly, that just would not be heaven. So when we cross over, our departed loved ones say, "Isn't it great we went together?" And we reply, "Yes!"

I don't know how others read or what information they receive, but this is my experience and my relationship with the other side. They can feel a certain date that may be coming up, but I believe they do this by sensing the time of year or seasons. I also believe they sense it from their loved ones who are sitting in front of me. They don't seem to understand the significance of the date, but they somehow know it is important to their person sitting with me.

So, I'm thinking that time has never really been important to me because I spent most of it with my friends on the other side. Given the history of my childhood all the way into adulthood, I feel it safe to say that I probably spend more time there than I do here. I truly do not like to be hurried, and I really don't care if I'm a bit late. I am not late to a fault, and I would never be rude, but I just can't get a hold of the hurry thing. It places me into some sort of meltdown mode. And I never understood why until I opened my first session's room and really began to spend time openly with my invisible friends not having to hide *who* and *what* I was any longer. Well, sort of.

Chapter Seventeen

My Calling

For Heaven's Sake—Answer the Phone!

IN JANUARY 2006, almost a year after my mother's death, I knew I had to do something that was going to truly turn my entire life upside down—AGAIN! I also knew that this upside down thing would eventually pass. OK, I didn't really *know* it; I *hoped* it would with all I had in me!

I simply woke up one morning with a plan. No, more like a *knowing*. I had to quit my job as a recruiter and open a session's room so that I could be available for strangers to heal the heart and the mind. I had to! Now, I had no clue as to how I was going to accomplish this *calling*, but I could have no more ignored this feeling than I could have ignored an elephant on my toe!

So, once again, I began to manifest. I knew in my heart of hearts and my knowing of all knowings that there just had to be a way to create a space, a safe and secure place for others to come where they could receive guidance, meet their Angels, and talk to their deceased loved ones. I knew it had to be beautiful, serene, and Angelic. This uncreated space had to embrace the person's very soul. It had to be private and confidential. Bottom line was: it just had to be!

I had received many readings during my plight to find out what in the Sam Hill was wrong with me throughout the years of my searching, and I never felt as though I could relax enough to even hear what the reader was telling me because the space lacked privacy and embracement. There were too many distractions. I would sit at a table in a spiritual book store with the reader across from me at a table while others were walking around behind me, talking and shopping. This did not work for me at all. I always ended up reading the reader. I didn't mean to, it just happened every time. Another sign, I suppose.

So in my quiet time or chore time or driving time, or whatever time my mind was left by itself unattended—which is quite dangerous for someone such as myself—I created a beautiful room in my mind, over and over and over again. My room! My space! My very own reading room! I was so excited, and yet I had no clue as to how I would accomplish this task or even where I would find such a place. However, my Angels told me to be patient, it would come. OK, me? Be patient? What a hoot! And then—one day—out of the blue—it happened!

I was sitting in my little office at home, working on the placement for a construction company, when my phone rang and on the other end of the line was a friend of mine who had worked for me while I was in staffing. She had decided to take another route a few years later and became a manicurist, but we had remained close friends.

The first question out of her mouth was, "Do you read cards?"

"What do you mean?" I asked her. "Like tarot cards?"

"Yes," she said, "isn't that what you do?"

"Uh no," I replied. "I have never held a deck of tarot cards in my life." Then I added, "I have Angel cards. Why, does someone need an Angel card reading?"

"Well, no," she said. "What exactly do you do? I mean, what are you?"

Huh, good question, I thought. I have no clue what I am, but I'm something.

"Well," I told her, and out of my mouth came the words as though I knew what I was talking about, and yet I had never spoken those words before in my entire life. "I am an Angelic Communicator and a medium," I told her.

"Perfect," she said. "The lady who owns the salon where I work is looking for someone like you to rent a room on the spa side of our salon. You know—someone kind of Spiritual, someone to help others. I told her about you, and she asked me to call you."

I was paralyzed with fear and excitement all at once. I felt that *knowing* knot in my stomach punch me so hard I was almost giddy.

"Is there a room?" I asked.

"Yes," she said, "everyone has their own room."

Oh my gosh—my own room with a closed door and everything!

"How much?" I asked.

She wasn't sure, but she gave me the owner's phone number and told me to call her.

Long after she hung up, I simply sat there staring at that phone number, just knowing that once I made that call there would be no stopping what would indeed be taking place. So, I just sat there a little longer, stunned and scared to death. This was it! I was about to commit to something I had only ever dreamed of. Then the fear and doubt began to creep in. How would I make a living doing this? How could I make rent on a room when I had no idea as to where my clients would come from? What would I charge? *Pick up the phone!* What was I really? Could I honestly do this? *Pick up the phone!* What if I was wrong? What if I did a reading and I was wrong? What if I really wasn't hearing Angels and the dead and I was crazy? What if that precious Doreen Virtue person had been wrong? What if she simply wanted to make a crazy person feel sane? What if a bolt of lightning hit me at that very minute and killed me deader than a doornail! *Pick up the gosh darn Godforsaken phone, Marti!*

I picked up the phone and hit the green button, and there was no dial tone! I had forgotten to hang it up and I never even heard that annoying beep, beep, beeping or that lady's voice telling me that if I'd like to make a call, please hang up and try your call again. *Now* where had I been?

I dialed the number I had jotted down, and a woman answered the phone.

I began to explain who I was, and before I could even finish, she interrupted me and exclaimed she was elated that I had called! I was stunned! I surely wasn't accustomed to being received with open arms—or such an open mind as to what I was, *whatever in the heck that was*, that was for sure! As a matter of fact, I wasn't even sure myself as to *what* exactly I was but I was about to find out!

"Can you come in today and look at the room?" she asked.

Uh today? Let's see, no, that probably won't work because I have some hot fire pits to walk through after I tread on some broken glass, and I think I will probably be busy for the rest of my pitiful life for that matter, so thanks for the offer, but I just can't do this right now because I couldn't move if my rear was on fire!

"Sure," I said. *What in the heck was I doing?*

"Perfect," she said. "Anytime today is fine. Just come in and ask for me. I will show you the room."

"How much is it?" I asked, hesitantly.

She told me not to worry about that. We would make it work until I got on my feet. And that was it! Not only had my Angels arranged my opening, but they wouldn't take no for an answer. My timing, *their* timing—was now! So, I grabbed my car keys and headed for the door.

All the way there I spoke to my Angels and God. Is this what I was asking for? Is it time? How will I know what to do? Do I call what I do reading? Oh snap! I was so confused and yet, I knew exactly what to do. Just get a person in front of me. Instead of keeping it to myself, it was time to verbally report!

I knew of the salon where my friend worked. It was beautiful. And the location was well known. I had not ever been on the spa side until that day. And it too was very quiet, professional, beautiful, and very inviting. All the massage therapists were on that side of the salon.

As I pulled into the parking lot, it already felt routine, just as though I had been doing it for years. It felt like home.

The owner was a real nice gal. Very friendly and extremely interested in me and *my gift!* Wow, for the first time ever, I didn't feel like a freak! She welcomed me with open arms.

She led me to the other side of the salon until we came upon an empty room with a sink and fluorescent overhead lighting. The walls needed painting and the floor was just a simple tile floor. Linoleum to be exact, and I truly hate linoleum, but none of what I was looking at seemed to matter. I loved it! I knew what Lindy and I could do to this room. We had been talking about it for years!

"I'll take it," I said. "Is there something I need to sign?" Like a lease or *perhaps my death certificate?*

"No," she said. "I don't need a lease. Let's just go month to month so you can feel more comfortable. So is the first of February OK?" she asked. *Huh, let me check my calendar. Uh—well—the first of February is looking OK for me and mostly because I have nothing, and I mean nothing, on my books whatsoever at all! Except for the fact that I have given myself only two weeks to do something I have never done before in my life! That's the only problem really. No need to panic.*

And that was it. I had just rented my first session's room, and I had no clue what a session even was! I wrote her a check for $550, which is what we agreed upon, and I never even thought twice about it—and I didn't have the $550 to play with! But I wasn't worried. I knew that this is where God wanted me, and I knew he would take care of my rent. I felt it. It was a *knowing*! It was time for me to have faith! And I may have fallen short in a lot of areas in my life but faith sure as heck wasn't one of them. I have always had strong faith that all is in divine order, and I always will!

I was scared to death when I left the salon that day. How was I going to explain this one to good old Bob? Poor guy. I brought home everything under the sun that no spouse should ever have to deal with. Kids, animals, and now this! What in the world had I been thinking? I needed to turn my car around, go back and get my check, and tell that nice lady that I had made a terrible mistake! Who did I think I was? What in the name of God did I think I was doing? But I didn't turn my car around and go back. No, I surely did not. My mind was reeling with how I was going to decorate that room to make it a sanctuary. I had to call Lindy!

That evening, Bob came home as usual, and I had prepared dinner—most *un-usual, (I hate to cook)*—and after I put the boys to bed, I grabbed a bottle of wine and two glasses, and we went out back to our deck to sit in the hot tub.

The crisp January air was biting but it felt good to sit in the heated tub and what? What was I doing? What was I going to say? How was I going to say it?

Bob was relaxing with his head back listening to music when I broke the silence, announcing to him that I had something I needed to tell him. In all honesty, I *did* think about telling him that I had adopted two more children or that I had committed a murder first so that when I told him the actual truth he would be relieved. Funny how our minds work when we are scared gutless, isn't it?

He sat up, giving me his undivided attention. He was probably thinking: Now what? What has she done this time? And for some truly apparent reason at that very moment, I felt like Lucy Ricardo!

I began by reminding him of my becoming ordained and then taking my seminary courses, as I thought I saw him almost yawn before I dropped the bomb.

I rented a session's room today, and I'm going to conduct readings, I said just as easy as you please. That came out well. Like water off a duck's back, which was very fitting, as we were, after all, in the hot tub.

Nothing. Dead silence. I looked him square in the eyes, and he had no expression. Nothing!

My Gosh, I had finally done it! I had talked my husband into a coma!

After a minute or ten of silence, I finally asked him to say something.

"Well," he said, "I really don't know what to say, babe. I don't know what the demand for that sort of thing is. Supply and demand." That was his retail way of thinking. His business sense.

"Well," I answered, "if you're the real deal, it is huge." *(Babe)*

"And are you the real deal?" he asked.

I sat there for just a second before I replied, "Yes, I am the real deal." And just as soon as I said that statement, I felt like a liar.

What if I wasn't the real deal, and what if all I had ever done thus far was become a great guesser? What if?

"Well then," he said, breaking my brainstorming conversation between me, myself, and I, "I guess all we have to lose is the first month's rent. Do you have an idea what you want to do with the room?"

Oh my gosh—I had been waiting years to create that room! I envisioned it in my mind over and over again. It would be a haven! It would be private and beautifully Angelic. It would be created just for my clients. A special place where they could come to escape the outside world. A most wonderful place of peace and serenity. Oh yes, I had quite an idea what I wanted to do with that room!

"Yes," I said. "It should be very simple and inexpensive to do."

"When?" he asked. "When are you planning on starting?"

Oh yeah, I guess I forgot to share that part with him, didn't I? Well, I was actually starting in about two weeks give or take. And no—I hadn't a clue where to begin buying furniture and Angels for my new room. Nor did I have a clue as to how I was going to find my clients. I really just didn't have a clue! But I knew it would happen. I knew I would hit the ground running. I felt it. I felt it with my entire being! That Doreen Virtue person had confirmed that I could do it! And she wouldn't have lied to me! I knew she meant what she had said.

"Well," I answered, "I'd like to be ready by the first of February." And that was that!

By the first of February 2006, with the help of Bob and Lindy, my very first session's room was beautiful and ready. Ready for *what*—was the question!

Chapter Eighteen

Doubts

If Doubts Were Pennies—I'd Be Rich!

DURING THE FOLLOWING two weeks, I became a nervous wreck. OK, I was already a nervous wreck. I mean that I became *more* of a nervous wreck. Who would have ever "thunk" that could have even been possible at that point in time? Well, if you are me, anything is possible!

I wasn't nervous about getting the room ready. I seemed to know exactly what I needed, and Lindy I went and got it all. From the candles right down to the Angles and the beautiful wicker furniture, my space looked like a little sitting room right out of a *Better Homes and Gardens Magazine*. But something else began tugging at me, and it was quite important actually. And it had to do with money.

I knew what other people were charging around town to do a reading, but they were card readers, and I didn't want to charge for my gift. But if I didn't charge for my readings, then I would have to continue to work a regular job. Oh my goodness, if there was ever a needle in a haystack, I would absolutely be the one to find it! I would probably sit directly on top of it!

Well, low and behold, just a couple of days before I was to open for business, I had a dentist appointment. My dentist is not only a woman, but she has also come to know me very well over the years, and I love her dearly.

So, there I sat, in the dentist's chair that day, waiting for her to come in and make my heart rate go up, and in she did come. She was excited for me when I told her I was finally going to fulfill my calling. However, she could also tell I was reserved and doubtful.

"You must be so excited," she said as she sat down on her little roller chair and scooted towards me.

"I am," I said reluctantly.

"What is wrong?" she asked. "I can tell you are struggling with something, Marti. What is it?"

"I don't feel right about charging for my gift, Mary," I said to her nearly in tears. "I just don't think it is right."

She sat there for just a second before she scooted closer to me. She placed her ever so caring hand on my arm and said, "Marti, you aren't charging for your gift, you are charging for your time. That is what we all do. We have to charge for our time. If you don't, then how ever will you be there for strangers? You have to make a living," she added.

"I don't know," I replied. Sounds like a trick of the mind to me. And it did. But why in the world would my longtime professional friend try to trick me?

"You want to be there for those who need you, right?" she asked.

"Yes," I said. "That is why I am doing this."

"And you have to make a living as well because you are not independently wealthy, are you?" she asked with a smile.

"Not hardly," I replied.

"Then if you don't charge for your time, you are going to have to work another job, which will defeat your purpose of everything you have dreamed of doing," she said. "Fulfilling your calling."

So I really thought about that statement long and hard as she worked on me that day. When I left, I got in my car and spoke to God. As we already know, I always talk to God in my car. It is quiet and safe. And I didn't just talk to God that day; I made a promise to God.

"OK," I said, "here's the deal, God. I will charge for my time, and I will do the very best I can to do what is right and what I am led to do—BUT—I will never turn anyone away because of their inability to pay." And that felt *so right*. I felt satisfied with a knowing that only he could fulfill. And I have never wavered. If someone cannot afford to pay, I see them anyway. Once I began this practice, something truly amazing happened. Others, who *could* afford to pay more, paid more, which made up for those who couldn't afford to pay. Miraculous! Truly miraculous indeed!

After getting that little ditty out of the way, I was ready to conduct my first reading in my new session's room, whatever the heck that meant, because I surely had no way of knowing until it happened, and happen *it did!*

I went in on the first day of February and sat in my room with the door open. I wondered—prayed—for whatever or whomever was to come my way.

I had placed fliers all around the salon. Then, I simply sat in my serenity room and waited. And on that day, one of the gals from the other side of the salon wandered over to my room, tapped lightly on the door, and she wanted to schedule a reading. My very first appointment had been booked and I was scared to death. This was it! She came to my room and made the appointment, and I scheduled her in. So this was *really* it. It was show time! And that reading was so powerful and so healing that that was all it took to push me into knowing that I really and truly *was* meant to be a healer of the heart and the mind. I amazed myself, and I amazed her. I can honestly say that with every reading after that, to this very day, I am still truly amazed and shocked at what comes out of my mouth, which makes me forever grateful every day of my life! There wasn't a doubt in my heart or my mind anymore. I was *indeed* a spiritualist and I was finally right where I belonged!

Chapter Nineteen

Additional Gifts

No Returns!—No Refunds!

I HAVE MOVED the location of my session's room seven times in eight years since that first reading at the salon. I usually get a notion or a sign that it is time to move on. I could have never dreamed that this would be part of the process, but it most certainly has been. Every one of my rooms has led me to another. Doesn't make a bit of sense to me, but it feels right, and I always know when it is time to move on. And I hate moving!

After that first reading, I learned so much that I couldn't have imagined what was in store for me had it been shown to me on paper in black and white!

First of all, I had abilities that I never really knew I had. Once I opened myself up to reading another person, all sorts of information came pouring in. I was confused but I somehow understood. Having the courage to report is the key. And I must say, I still freeze up at times, and I'm afraid to share the information.

I can see pictures like a movie or memories that are not my own. Like in the beginning of this story when I saw that child's murder. I can describe the inside of someone's home, right down to the color of the walls or the type of flooring. I can see boxes of pictures in closets, and I can see what is in those boxes. I can see out windows in someone's home and describe what is in the front or back yard. And I can see illness. I know if someone is sick or if they need to have something looked at. And although this is most perplexing to me, it never stops me from speaking my knowing. My belief is that if I get a warning, we are allowed to change it; otherwise, I wouldn't get it. And sometimes I don't get it. *They* don't always tell me. We have free will, but we cannot stop fate.

I do not see the inside of the human body like a doctor would. Organs are not exactly where they should be, and I see everything in color. I have learned that if I see white—it is an old injury. I can see if someone has had a stroke because it shows up like a white starburst at the base of the brain, like a tiny little sun shining. I see an aneurism as a bigger yellow sunshine. If I get a small yellow starburst at the base of the brain on the right side, it means memory loss. If I see black fuzziness, it is cancer. Those on the other side call this poison. I can see the blood flow as a river. If I see slow blood flow through the legs, it is almost always heart. If I get a yellow starburst anywhere in the body, it is a warning. And I learned all this from the deceased. Yes, they have explained to me what I was seeing. They are my true teachers.

I don't usually get names when I talk to the other side. I simply ask them who they are to the person sitting in front of me and I ask them how they died. Sometimes they will offer a name but I don't get bent out of shape if they don't. The deceased always know how they died. And they are very specific. I don't allow the client to tell me anything but yes or no until their Angels tell me that they trust me completely. Then I will allow them to elaborate on certain things to save time. Until the client knows beyond a shadow of a doubt that I have who they are looking for, I ask questions and allow them to answer me with only yes and no. Validation is everything, and I don't ever want someone to feel tricked. I tell my clients they should never give a spiritualist information. They should wait and allow the spiritualist to give the information to *them*!

I have strict guidelines in my session's room, such as: I do not allow tape recorders. I would feel like I was exploiting my children! I'm not a show boat, and I don't need to be validated on tape. I ask my clients to take notes if need be. Nothing happens so fast during my readings that one cannot take notes.

I do not and would not allow the media in a session, and I really can't ever imagine conducting a reading with a camera rolling. What happens in that session's room is private and confidential. I am dealing with a person's emotional feelings regardless of why they have come to me and it is not to be taken lightly in any way. Sometimes, depending on the circumstances, I cry right along with my client, especially if we are dealing with the death of a child. Those are the toughest for me. I just don't know how someone can continue breathing after such a loss, and I tell my clients exactly that. The human heart has got to be the strongest organ in our bodies. It can be shattered into a million pieces and it can still continue to keep beating. It can be broken into shards of remains that a forensics team could not put back together. Yet it can still love again, and it can actually still love the person who broke it in the first place. Truly amazing and miraculous!

If my client isn't satisfied with a reading, he or she doesn't pay. It is that simple. I have ever only stopped two readings in my eight years of doing this. The first time, I stopped because I could not move what I felt was an Angel. I asked and I asked, but it felt huge and it wouldn't budge. Therefore, I couldn't conduct the reading because of fear. My fear! I wasn't sure what or whom I was dealing with, so I quit. And then another time was because the client continued to argue with everything I said, so I felt it a waste of time for both of us to go on.

I surely don't know everything, and I learn something new every time I conduct a reading. This world is full of the unknown and I try to learn as much as I can each and every day.

I feel extremely blessed in that I have established quite a relationship with those on the other side. I depend on them for so much that if I don't get a warning just before something happens, I have to take a step back and remember that I get only what they can give. For this I am truly thankful! I love meeting new people from the other side. I love the feeling they surround me with, and I love to feel the embrace that only the deceased can give. It makes me feel safe.

I have been forewarned of a plane crash, but had no clue when it was going to happen or even if it was going to happen until it did. I had a location and how it would go down. That was it. Who in the world would I report something like that to anyway?

I have been forewarned of many heart attacks, and all I can say about that is that their Angels must have prearranged that person getting to me in order for me to have told them. It wasn't their time to go, and I was the messenger they used to give the warning. And if not me, it would have been someone else. If they need to warn us, they will certainly find a way. Everything is in Divine Timing and Divine Order.

I have felt and reported cancer in a person's body and one of the saddest of those instances was a very close friend of mine who came in to see me one day. She reached across and touched my hand and, embarrassingly, I pulled my hand back. Out of my mouth came the words, "Oh my gosh, you have cancer in your body!" Then I realized what I had just indeed said, and I put my hands over my mouth, apologizing for what I had just said. She already knew, and that is why she had come to see me that day. I felt terrible. She began extensive treatments and we spent many good times together out on my back porch where she could take off her wig or her scarf, exposing her beautiful bald head. We drank wine together, and she relaxed and allowed the afternoon sun to kiss her cheeks as she gazed at the mountains. She would come and sit for hours. It was her private sanctuary. She fought that damned cancer for a couple of years until it finally won. But not before she begged for me to write this book and tell my story. At the time I said I would just to appease her. I had no intention of telling my story. Perhaps she was the very reason I simply decided to sit down one day and start typing. She called me her Angel. I miss her dearly.

I have been awakened by those from the other side in the middle of the night with warnings or messages for loved ones, and I have been known to make a phone call or two at three o'clock in the morning just so I can sleep. Those on the other side can be relentless until a message has been delivered. So I suppose we could say that they depend upon me just as much as I depend upon them. They know I will deliver a message no matter how much it doesn't make sense at the time. And yes, sometimes I still doubt myself to this day, but I always report what I hear. No matter what!

Some messages are happy, such as the birth or conception of a new life. Those on the other side love to share the news of a new life coming into our world. And just as readily, they do not hesitate to tell me when someone is leaving soon. That makes them just as happy. Go figure!

All in all, my journey, my knowing, or my gift, as it has been called, has been a blessing. And I do feel blessed! Well, most of the time anyway.

Chapter Twenty

My Journy's End

We Just Took—A Sentimental Journey!

WELL, WE ARE now at the end of my story. Well, whatever "the end" means. Up until the point of the ending of this book, I suppose.

I have learned so very much throughout the years, and as I shared with you earlier, I continue to learn more every day. (Thank God or whomever you choose to thank.)

My gift becomes stronger every day. I learn more about how to communicate, shortcuts so to speak, and sometimes, I still like to take the long way home! It just feels right.

There are days when I wish I could quit. Oh yes, there have been many of those! However, this is a calling, not a job. Therefore, I could no more walk away from this than I could walk right out of my own body! It just wouldn't work. I would feel like something was missing. And it would be. *Them!*

I get frustrated on some days during certain readings, and I feel disappointed in myself at times. I either feel like I could have done better or I should have gotten a certain something that didn't happen to come out in a reading. Ah, but there are also those days when I feel like I am on top of the world because I got more than I ever bargained for! The true kicker is: I have never been able to determine why. Why some readings go far better than others. Perhaps I will never know. However, I know I am right where I am supposed to be doing exactly what I am supposed to be doing. God doesn't make mistakes. Sure wish I had all the answers. Perhaps I do and I just recited them. Who's to say?

I have been asked by many to share stories of my readings in this book. I was hesitant to do so until my friends and clients begged for just a couple of stories. The ones that are most prevalent in my memory. Well, those would have to be the ones that I will never forget. To be quite truthful, I may forget the client who was in my room, but I never forget the loved one on the other side. Strange, isn't it? So, I have, although reluctantly, decided to share just one reading that was dearest to me because of the healing it created, the truth it brought forward, and the mystery it unraveled. It brought peace to my client, who is now a very good friend of mine. She was honored that I asked her to share her reading. I am honored that her son Freddie trusted me enough to come to me and share what he did. He trusted *me* of all people to deliver a message to his mother. Her name is Carol Avalos and this is her story in her own words.

I came to know Marti when my son Frederick Robert Christian Franks hung himself in the garage of a home he and three roommates were renting from Freddie's father, Fred. A week or so after we buried him, a client for whom I had done previous electrical work called me requesting a job quote. Her name is Kathy, and I had taken Freddie over there to help me with some work, so she had met him before. Kathy also had a son who passed a year before Freddie. I told her Freddie had died, and she told me to come over the following Saturday to talk and look at the job. On Saturday I told Kathy how tortured Freddie's father and I were about the way Freddie had died, as he always promised us he would never kill himself. We just couldn't understand why he did this. Kathy told me about a medium named Marti Tote who lived in Reno who did a reading for her. Kathy suggested I call Marti for a reading in hopes she could solve this mystery and bring us some peace. Strange as it is, Kathy never called me back for the job.

I called Marti that day when I got home from Kathy's. Although Marti doesn't normally do phone readings, when she heard the urgency in my voice, she agreed to do a reading the following Friday at 1:00 p.m. Marti told me to allow at least two hours. Before we hung up, I asked Marti if she needed a picture or anything. Marti told me, "No, I don't want to know anything about you. I know your first name and that is all I need. Talk to you Friday." I was so anxious by the time Friday came, my nerves were on edge. At promptly 1:00 p.m., the phone rang and the caller ID said "Marti Tote." We started out talking about such things as the weather in Riverside and Reno, when all a sudden the phone went dead. I frantically tried to call her back, but could not get through. I immediately burst into tears. Later, I learned she had been trying to call me back also, but a storm in her area had knocked out phone service. Later that afternoon, Marti was finally able to call me back. She told me because it was so late, she would do the reading the next day at 1:00 p.m., even though she doesn't normally do readings on Saturdays.

Saturday at 1:00 p.m., Marti called again. She explained the way the reading was to go by telling me not to give any information or details, but to answer only yes or no unless she specifically asked. Marti also told me that a lot of times, for reasons unknown to even her, when a question is asked of an entity, they won't answer. She says it's because for some reason, we're not supposed to know the answer. They are only allowed to tell us so much. She was quiet for a moment and then began to ask me questions and tell me details.

Marti: I feel that you've recently had a child who has passed. Oh, my God, I hate it when it's a child—these are the most difficult readings. I'm sorry. Is this true?
Carol: True.
Marti: I get the feeling of a female.
Carol: No.
Marti: OK—when I feel this way, it doesn't necessarily mean it is a girl or that it's a boy who is feminine, if it is a boy, it normally means he was into the arts more than, say, sports and such (long pause). Oh my God! This was a—hanging! Why? Why would you do this? What's his name, please? Can I have his name?

Carol: Freddie—That's why I'm here—I need to know why. I want to know where he is.

Marti: Ask him yourself. He can hear you, Carol. Freddie! Why would you hang yourself?

Carol: Freddie, where are you?

Marti: He's saying—"Mom, I'm fine—I'm on the other side. Everyone's here. Mom, I'm sorry. I love you. What's the big deal?"

Carol: What's the big deal? You rip my heart out and you say, "What's the big deal?"

Marti: OK, he's taken me into a building like a garage or something. It's higher in the center of the building, like the roof area, than it is on the sides. It's dark in there, no windows, but there's light coming in from above.

Carol: True.

Marti: There's some type of motorcycles along one wall. There's a car, something dark back in there.

Carol: No.

Marti: Yes—there is! It's a car, or some kind of vehicle. I see him standing on it!

Carol: There's Sea-Doos.

Marti: Is there a dark cover on them?

Carol: Yes.

Marti: There are footprints in the dust on the cover of the Sea-Doos where he was standing on them. There's a lot of cat hair on the cover too. Look at it. You will see the footprints!

Carol: That's true. He was caring for his friend's cat the week before he died. He hated the hair it shed. I'm sorry my oldest daughter took the Sea-Doos to the lake yesterday. It's probably all washed away. I'll check.

Marti: He's telling me that before he had come here, before he was born, God asked him if he wanted to take the life—that it was going to be short—and he said that he did. So he knew he wasn't going to be here long. He wants you to know that we all go to the same place, so don't worry. He wants to know how long he's been gone.

(Marti talking to Freddie)—"Three weeks. No, hon, OK, not even a season."

Marti: He doesn't understand the concept of time. There's no time on the other side. I have to explain it in seasons. They seem to understand what a season is. Freddie has five groups of friends. School friends, Work friends, Rave friends, Childhood friends, and friends from the Dredge. He's saying, "I didn't know I was gone from there until I saw my own funeral. It was huge, and it was as big as the president's." He says it's like watching TV with a regular picture, but he gets it that he's not here anymore. Did he smoke? I swear to you when I sat down out here to call you, he sat down on the bench right beside me, and I can clearly smell cigarette smoke.

Carol: That's true. We expected two hundred people. Six hundred showed up. Yes, he smoked.

Marti: He's saying he had a girlfriend, but that was over with a long time ago, and that's not the reason this happened.

Carol: OK, we were blaming her because he was texting with her and talking to her the night before he died.

Marti: No, that was over. He was done with that before he moved. He's telling me he worked on the water with his father, around loud machines. He says he loves the ocean.

Carol: That's true.

Marti: He says he also loves the desert. (Marti talking to Freddie)—"How can you love the ocean AND the desert? You have to love either one or the other." (laughs)

Carol: That's true, he did love both. He loved to ride in the desert. (crying)

Marti: (talking to Freddie)—"I know, dear. No, I can't do anything. No, she's not hurt. Her heart is hurt. She misses you! She'll be OK." (Marti explaining to me)—"There's no emotional pain or sadness on the other side. When you cry, he thinks you're in pain or you're physically hurt, and he wants me to help you. He keeps telling me to do something to make you stop crying. I have to explain to him that you are hurt because you miss him, but it's hard. They don't understand this."

Carol: OK.

(*long pause*)

Marti: He's asking me, "Will she always cry like this?" (*Marti talking to Freddie*)—"She cries because she can't see you. She doesn't know where you are." He wants me to tell you, "Mom, I'm on the other side. Just close your eyes and you can see me."

Carol: I am, and I can't—(*still crying*).

Marti: Yes, you will. He will show himself in other ways. OK, Carol, sometimes just to prove to you that they are who they say they are to you, they will say funny things that only you would know. It's validation. So, here goes, just to prove this really is your son talking to me, he's telling me you like to clean the house wearing your nightshirt, and it grossed him out.

Carol: Yes, that's true (*laughing*). He always finds a way to make me laugh.

Marti: He's saying, "Mom, tell Dad I know he's thinking of selling the bikes. Tell Dad, not to stop doing what he does, don't stop riding. Don't sell them. I can ride with him again. I have memories of riding." He's saying he gets lots of flashbacks of camping.

Carol: That's true, he camped a lot.

Marti: He's saying he has a big family, a lot of sisters.

Carol: Yes, that's true.

Marti: One sister is pretty quiet.

Carol: Yes, that's Lora.

Marti: Another is loud, a funny one. She's with child.

Carol: That's Leslie. No, she's not pregnant.

Marti: Yes, he says she is, and he's met the child. He wants you to tell them he's OK.

Carol: I will.

Marti: I can feel he has a dog with him there. He's saying, "Mom, I slipped, I'm sorry. I was dicking around and I slipped. I love you, I'm sorry." He keeps showing me his arm, Carol, the right one. There's something on it. I can't tell what it is. Did he have a tattoo?

Carol: No. Freddie didn't like tattoos. He didn't like it when I got mine.

Marti: He keeps saying, "my arms" and showing me his forearms. I can't tell what that is on it. He's saying he's sorry, he slipped.
Carol: I don't know.
Marti: You know, Carol, I don't get the feeling this is a suicide. I've had many readings of suicides and I always get this "Oh shit" feeling. I'm not getting that here. I'm thinking this was somehow an accident. You wouldn't believe the number of deaths ruled suicide that are, accidents. It's more than you know.
Carol: He said he'd never kill himself. He promised. He didn't have anything to do it for, but we didn't know how else it could have happened. This explains a lot. It makes sense.
Marti: Carol, He says for you to get the paper, the report on the fourth page at the bottom, you will see where he injured his right arm trying to save himself. He says he was wasted, screwing around, trying to scare his friends. He's saying he got the mark on his arm trying to grab the rope to save himself. Carol, can you get the report?
Carol: I don't know. I will call and ask.
Marti: Please, when you get it, will you mail it to me?
Carol: Yes.

The day after this reading, my daughter Leslie came by my house and told me she had taken a test that morning and she was pregnant. The following Monday I called the coroner's office and talked to the sergeant. I asked him if I could get a copy of my son's death report. He said he would send me a copy as soon as it was finished. Three weeks later, there was a copy in my mailbox. I opened it and immediately turned to the fourth page. In the last paragraph it said, "Other injuries: 1-1/2" abrasion to the inside of the right forearm." My son slipped, just as he said he did.

My Account and What I Heard on my End:

Carol was referred to me by another client as everyone who finds me is, as I do not advertise. I received a call from her asking for a phone reading. I hate phone readings or I should say I did before this one. They just don't seem as personal or I should say again, until this one. So we set up a time and a day, and I called her.

When I first called her, our phones lost the connection, just as she said. We tried again and again and continued to lose our connection. I was truly ready to just call it quits as I was taking this as a sign. I did not remember rescheduling for that Saturday.

When I got the urge to walk outside, it was odd for me, as I love my session's room. But I walked outside my room for whatever reason and sat on the beautiful marble bench I had placed there, truly thinking that the phone reception might be better. Boy was that an understatement!

Just as I got her on the phone, I felt someone clearly walking, and very quickly, I might add, down the sidewalk toward me from my right side. However, I saw no one, but the person absolutely sat right down next to me on that bench! I had already given her the rundown as to the yes and no answers only, when I heard and felt this energy say to me: I'm her child! I immediately froze up inside just like I always do when I feel a child on the other side but this one was a bit different. He told me to relax and that he would tell me everything and not to be afraid. I did not feel male or female right away that I recall.

Tell her it was an accident. Tell her I didn't do it on purpose, he pleaded. *She needs to know!*

OK, I said to him in my mind, how did you die, son? (Carol had already confirmed it was her son)

I hung myself.

How in the heck do you accidentally hang yourself? I asked him in my mind. I was most perplexed, to say the least, and all the while with this woman on the other end of the line waiting for me to gather my thoughts. Just give me a minute, I told her. I have someone talking to me.

And he then told me this story word for word as he also showed me the entire scenario in my mind.

I was with my buddy, and we were drinking and playing video games. It was late, and I went out into the garage to have a cigarette. I got to thinking how it would be fun to scare the crap out of him when he came out looking for me, so I climbed up on the jet skis in the garage, and I moved the ladder close to me so I could get down safely. There was a rope, so I hung it around the beam and then I loosely placed it around my neck so that when he came out it would look like I was hanging there but the jet skis were underneath me. Ask her—she knows, he said excitedly—*my footprints were on the jet ski cover! But as I turned my head to the side to make it look like I was hanging, I slipped and lost my balance.*

First of all, this information comes to me in a millisecond all at once just like someone threw a snowball at me and all the information just splats throughout my knowing. So I don't get the pleasure of processing or even reading it like you just did. It is one thought and it comes very quickly as a knowing. This one just so happened to come with a viewing as well. Like a movie. So, there I sat with all that information, and I just knew it wasn't going to be good enough.

I had just one more detail to ask of him. I knew I could describe the garage and the jet skis, etc., as I could see everything clearly, even in black and white. But I also knew I needed more! This was a mother who lost her son to a hanging. Just because I could describe the death scene didn't make it *enough*. So I asked for more information. He knew what I needed. They always do.

Prove it, I said to him. I need more proof than this. Help me, I pleaded with him. Help me to help her! And that is when he said it. It's like finding the golden ticket! He told me that she hadn't gotten the paperwork back yet (meaning the autopsy report, I was assuming), and that in that report it would show that he had a bruise on the inside of his right arm between the wrist and the elbow where he tried to grab the rope to pull himself back up, but it was no use. He just couldn't lift his own weight. *You have to tell her,* he was pleading with me. *She thinks I left her on purpose!*

And then the questions began and the reading went on with me explaining several more times what I knew with her and both of us crying.

About three weeks later, I received an envelope in the mail. It was Freddie's autopsy report sent to me from Carol. And in that report, she highlighted an area at the bottom of the fourth page that read: "Other injuries: 1-1/2" abrasion to the inside of the right forearm."

And that was the beginning of a new relationship. And to this day, I still love to talk to Freddie, although as more time passes, he has less to say. Just seems to go that way sometimes.

That reading will always be one of my most cherished. He had to tell her the truth. She couldn't imagine why her son would have committed suicide. They were extremely close. He was her *youngest* and *only* boy in a four-girl household. There was nothing he couldn't tell his mom, and he was gone, leaving her with no explanation. What a horrible feeling. The whys of a death are hard enough, let alone the whys of a suicide. He had to find a way to get to her and he did!

Suicide, what a horrible-sounding word. I don't particularly care for it myself. Perhaps it is because when those who have taken their own lives come to me, they say they died suddenly, tragically, and unexpectedly. Then they tell me they had something to do with their own crossing over. And yes, they all come to me from the very same place as everyone else. As far as I know everyone goes to the same place. I have never been told any differently. I would imagine that because God doesn't make mistakes, he knew long before the thought of dying ever crossed their minds, how they were going to leave this place. That's another *DUH* in my knowing. It's all in the big plan. I have no clue as to why. And I think this is where we came in.

There is more conversation that takes place during a reading beyond what I have shared with you here of course. This reading was almost three hours long. But Carol chose to share only what she shared and gave me permission to do the same.

Readings are so unpredictable. Sometimes I get information that makes no sense to the person sitting in front of me, especially coming from those who have crossed over. In the beginning of my career conducting readings, this intimidated the heck out of me. I would get names that they would throw out at me, and when it meant nothing to my client, I would get frazzled, even knowing that I heard the names clearly. So, I stopped saying the names I was getting. It made me feel stupid and like a liar (once again). That is, until I met a client in about the third year of my profession. She was sitting in my room one afternoon and her brother, who was on the other side, continued to say the name Ruby. And he just wouldn't get off the name Ruby. She kept insisting that she knew no one by that name and I, once again, felt stupid and dumbfounded. However, this time I told my client that I know I was hearing the name clearly. I would not take it back because I couldn't. I had that knowing feeling in my gut and so I just left it alone as did she.

After she left my room that day she left me a message on my cell phone. She was so flabbergasted that I could barely understand what she was saying. It turns out that when she got in her car and checked her messages, there was a message from a receptionist on her own voice mail reminding her of an appointment she had booked for the next day. The receptionist's name was Ruby.

I suppose they do things like that to show the person that it is really them, that they are here. VALIDATION! That is all I can figure, because it happens more times than I care to mention. And I will say this as well: I have never not said a name since. If I hear it, I say it.

Who's to say why the other side does what they do? I have no clue. Some things make perfect sense later on and some don't. As I have said all along, I'm just a reporter. And I love who I interview. I get lost in the feeling of their comfort. They make me feel safe. And what I do makes me feel whole.

There are some folks out there in the world with more influential credentials than myself, who believe that everyone has this capability that I have shared with you throughout this story. This *gift*. They believe that anyone can do this. I simply believe in believing! So the question I will leave you with is this: Do you believe? It is a simple question, and yet it can get so very complicated. Belief is left up to every individual. So, does believing make it so? Only you can answer that question.

I have made reference to God throughout my story. I feel comfortable with calling my higher power by that name and referring to him as a he. I suppose that must have come from a tiny little girl, who went to church with her daddy in a land far away and long ago. However, you may call your higher power something completely different, and believe you me, there are many titles out there. I am thankful for this! We all have choices and different perceptions. I encourage you to follow your own path and your own knowing when it comes to such things. I am delighted that we are all individuals and we are all truly unique. What a blessing indeed!

I would wish you luck, but I don't believe in luck. I would wish you safe travels but I don't believe in wishes either. That pony wish did me in years ago! So I'm going to send you blessings! I will send a blessing for every person who reads this passage. *Do* you feel *them*? *Do* you hear *them*? *Can* you feel *them*? *Can* you hear *them*? Well, I believe you *can* if you will allow yourself to. Remember, you aren't listening for a voice—but for a soft and subtle "Whisper in the Wings!"

Epilogue

And so it has been written. A true story that reads like a fairy tale. One that I truly enjoyed sharing once I got started. It only took me fifty-six years to get there!

My gift has been an incredible journey. It has given me the opportunity to help so many people. And that is what truly makes me happy! Helping others.

I am no longer afraid to say *who* and *what* I am. I am a spiritualist, I am an Angelic Communicator, and I am a Medium. I hear those who have crossed over, and I am able to gift to their loved ones left behind, one more heartfelt conversation. One more message. One more I love you! Who can say they can do that for people every day? Not many!

I am a healer of the heart and the mind, and I feel blessed and honored that I was chosen for this prestigious position. I can hear people's Angels and they guide me to help them to find their way when they are lost. I can help them to find a new path in life. I can give them something substantial to hold onto and to believe in. I can help them to believe in themselves! Who can say they can do that every day? Again, not many.

I am also someone who loves and feels people from deep within their souls. I hurt when they hurt, and I cry when they cry. I'm extremely proud of that.

I have been told by some throughout the years, that I shouldn't get too close. That I should not get too personal with my clients. That I should keep my distance and not get too attached. How in the world could I ever NOT? Once I am connected to someone's Angels or their loved ones, I become adopted. I am family.

Every time I conduct a reading, what happens in my session's room is a miracle to me. It always will be! I have always believed in miracles, and I am so blessed to be a part of many miracles every day in so many ways.

I am finally right where I belong. It has been a long hard climb but so worth the effort because once I reached the top—the view was breathtaking! And it still is every day of my life!

I am thankful, I am blessed, I am gifted and I am me, Marti Tote. And now you know my story.

Thank you so much for accompanying me on my journey. My hope is that you enjoyed reading it as much as I enjoyed writing it. I don't have to be alone anymore. I have friends who understand me now—and I am whole and I am home!

About the Author

MARTI TOTE IS a spiritualist, medium, angelic communicator, and life coach who lives in Reno, Nevada. Her calling is to spiritually heal the heart and the mind. Her passion is her writing. Her peace and solace is the time spent with her horses. However, her most cherished moments are spending time with her husband, children, and grandchildren; for her strongest belief is in God and the very strength of family, as she believes that at the end of each and every day, all we really have is each other!

Made in the USA
Middletown, DE
02 January 2016